# The Player Slayer

**THE POCKET GUIDE TO JAMMING
THE PLAYER'S GAME**

*by*
"Ms. T."

AGATE
CHICAGO

Printed in Canada.

Library of Congress Cataloging-in-Publication Data
Ms. T.
    The player slayer : the pocket guide to jamming the player's game / by Ms. T.
        p. cm.
    Summary: "A humorous relationship guide on how to defeat, reject, and otherwise deflect the 'players' in your life"—Provided by publisher.
    ISBN-13: 978-1-932841-15-2 (pbk.)
    ISBN-10: 1-932841-15-6 (pbk.)
    1. Dating (Social customs) 2. Interpersonal relations.
I. Title.

    HQ801.M718 2006
    646.7'7—dc22

                                        2005017904

Agate books are available in bulk at discount prices. Single copies are available prepaid direct from the publisher.

Agatepublishing.com

THIS BOOK IS DEDICATED TO MY MOTHER,
THE LATE **JEAN D. SHAW.**

*It's finally our turn to win.*

# Table of Contents

# Introduction

PLAYED!!
AGAIN!!!

HOW'D IT HAPPEN? You've been through it before... and before... and before. But this time it was supposed to be different. You took your time. You weren't the first one to say, "I love you." You introduced him to your friends, and they approved. You waited two whole minutes before you let him hit it.

And he waited patiently. He did everything right. He gave you A CAR. Not the beep-beep kind. A-C-A-R (Affection, Consideration, Attention, Respect). He was with you on Thanksgiving, Christmas, New Year's Eve, and your birthday. He brought you gifts (and even wrapped them). He held your hand in public and hugged you when you went to the movies. He introduced you to his boys. Hell, he introduced you to his mother. And still he played you.

So now you're all broken up inside. You're sad and lonely and mad at yourself and you hate him. Stop. Stop right there.

*Don't Hate the Player, Hate the GAME.*

Nah. That's just a cliché—one that the players and the played alike use to keep the game in a cloud of smoke, hiding the fact that somebody played the game better than somebody else. Two people climbed in the ring. Somebody got their ass beat. It was you. Now you wanna hate the game. Did Tyson hate boxing when Buster Douglas whooped his ass? Did the Lakers hate basketball when they got beat down by the Spurs and the Pistons? Did you hate your momma when you got caught cutting school and she tore your butt up? No. You hated that fact that you got caught. That you didn't play the game better.

This book is about the game, and how you play it.

Now for those of you who feel that relationships are not or should not be a game, put this book down. For those who think that if you are reduced to having to play games, you'd rather be alone, then go ahead and *be* alone, and put this book down. And for those of you who feel that if he's a player, he's not worth your time; that you can spot a player a mile away and won't get caught up; that if you by chance find yourself involved with a player, well, you'll just make him change his playin' ways—for those of you who feel like that, then for God's sake PUT THIS BOOK DOWN!!!!! Go read *The Lord of the Rings*, or *Interview with the Vampire*, or *When a Black Man Loves*, or some other tale of fantasy.

But if you're honest with yourself, you may realize that some of the sweetest twists and turns you've ever had were on the player's ride. There was just something about that guy, and the one before him, and the one before him, that obviously attracted you. Something that just curled your toes. And whatever that something is, it'll probably be in the next mug you find yourself attracted to. You like what you like, but time and time again, that flavor you like is wrapped around a player.

If you just keep getting played and you're tired of it and ready to do something about it, then before you're played again, just stop what you're doing.

Pull up a chair. Put your comfy clothes on. Grab a cool lemonade or a hot cup of tea or a Mocha Frappuccino. Take my hand, open your mind, and prepare yourself for this eye-opening journey. Come with me as we enter the Land of The Game.

My name is Ms. T. And I'll be your guide. Now let's get to work!

# One ‖ Defining the Game

THE PURPOSE OF THIS BOOK is to show you how to keep from getting played. My aim is to provide the tools and information necessary to enable you to defend against the player's game, while not necessarily avoiding the player completely. But before we get to the mechanics of how to slay the player, we need to take a closer look at what we're up against. We need to understand the following:

- What is the game?
- How and why is the game played?
- Who plays the game?
- Who is the game played on?

Let's begin by defining the game and understanding its goals and objectives. Simply put, the goal or object of the game is to get the most while giving the least. To hit and not be hit. To get ass, but not bring ass. However, just as it's almost impossible to climb into a boxing ring with a worthy opponent and hit but not get hit, so it is that you cannot play the game without giving up something. There needs to be some exchange.

Now, while fair exchange is no robbery, the game is rarely ever played fair. And how can it be? There's no scale, no weigh station to determine the value of each individual's love, sex, time, sense of humor, ingenuity, et cetera. Furthermore, since the player believes himself to be just short of platinum, and thus whatever he shares with you is tantamount to a gift from the gods, then any of his slightest efforts are more than payment for your steadfast love and devotion. (Sorry: every now and again a little hate seeps out—I'll try to keep it in check).

One of the most important points to understand is this: the game is played very lopsidedly. The exchanges that take place aren't even. Somebody will give a lot and somebody will get a lot. *And that rule is not made clear at the onset of the game.* Actually, you're probably not aware of the unevenness of the game until you're well on your way to being played. Sure would have been nice to know the rules from the door, wouldn't it? Well, now you know. It ain't fair. So keep this in mind as one of the primary rules of the game.

So how is the game played? What does the player use as game pieces? Two things, nothing more: *Words* and *Deeds*. What is said and what is done. The degree to which both are used varies from player to player, from mark to mark, from situation to situation, and from moment to moment. But these are the player's tools. And his entire game is based on his usage of both: the timing and the output and the eventual minimizing of his words and deeds while maximizing what he acquires in return. Thus, as the player's game progresses, his objective is to reduce the words to as few as possible, and the deeds to even fewer, without losing any ground with his mark.

## Words
The words used are based on what the player's mark (the one who has been marked by the player as the person on whom he will play his game) wants and needs to hear at that particular time. These words

may all be nothing more than verbal garbage, or they may be colored with a tinge of legitimate honesty and sincerity. They might just be the player's usual rap, some words used in another scenario (one that worked) or even lines from an obscure book, movie, or song. Note: when the player starts quoting Luther's hits, you know you're in for some raggedy game.

However, the words may even come directly from the player's soul. They may capture what he truly feels, wants, or dreams. For example, someone once told me, "I know he's a player, but he spoke to me with such honesty and depth about his problems with his mother that I felt him. I mean I really felt him. I don't think he shares that part of himself with just anyone. I must be special to him."

So what—he shared! He has real feelings about something (not you—don't get it twisted) and he shared them. Does it mean that since he opened up to you, your relationship with him is different from every other relationship he had—or has? Does it mean that he's found the girl of his dreams, and he can now change his evil ways because you are the ammunition he's always needed (and never found until now) to fight the good fight? No. It only means he told you about his problems with his mother. Why? Maybe he needed to get it off his chest. Maybe he was preparing to talk to a family member about it and was using you as a sounding board. Maybe he needed to get to the personal sharing zone with you, that place where he (seemingly) opens himself up to you and expects you to do the same. Whatever the reasons, they're his reasons. You'll probably never know what they are, and so what! You don't need to know.

What you do know is that *all he did was to say some words.* That's it. He will say many more words. And why shouldn't he? They come out of a dictionary and they are free to use. He can say what he pleases and he probably will. They may be sweet words or words designed to cut out your heart, but they're all just words. That's it. Just. Words. They don't feed you or clothe you. They don't pay your bills or fix your car. They don't buy you gifts or escort you to your cousin's wedding. They don't kiss you and, with the exception of some good phone sex, they don't get you off.

But words do have a function. They are used by the player to make you think he actually just *did* something, when in reality all he did was *say* something. And they can be used in the same way by you, too! Words are free, and they really can't hurt you unless you let them. Remember that "sticks and stones" stuff your momma told you? It's really true.

The thing about the word game is that we either dismiss it too quickly as a bunch of empty promises or else we put way too much stock in it. We quickly recognize "Baby I'm gonna stop, drop, and give you the world" as game because it's so overt. When it reeks of fantasy, it probably is fantasy. But how about the subtle lines? One of my all-time favorite lines is, "We should try to see each other more often." It says so much, and generally works like a charm (yep, it got me good a few times). It says, "I like your company. Whatever else I have going on in my life, I want to make room for more of you. I'm putting my feelings out there for you to bear witness to." But what it probably means is "Cancel everything on your plate and sit back and wait for me to spend more time with you." The face value of these words, "We should try to see each other more often," is just a statement based on what? Again, who knows? It does not require any action, any plan-changing or rearranging, any drawer-cleaning or toothbrush-buying on your part. Lines like these don't require much of a response from you—a single nod should suffice, to acknowledge that you do in fact recognize the English language when spoken.

You have to understand the word game for what it is: this is essential to countering the player's game. Most of what we do *wrong* when encountering the game is done because of our response to words. Words make up more than half of the game in the beginning, and more than 95 percent of it when the game is being played at its best. The word game lifts us up and breaks us down. Makes us beautiful and ugly, confident and insecure. It confuses us and makes us lose control.

We'll talk about the strategy for dealing with the word game in more detail a little further down the line. But until you've finished reading this book, run to the store and get some earplugs. Keep the players out of your ears for now. Tell them you're too busy to talk. Make up any excuse, whatever you need to tell them, just keep them out of your ears for now. You need to concentrate on the lesson at hand. Don't worry, they'll still be there with plenty of shit to say when you pull the plugs out. They know you need and want to hear it. Just dying to hear it. Can't wait to hear it. They'll put that shit on ice, keep it fresh and cool for you, so you can hear it later as a personal favor to you. And you betta know it's a favor to you, Sista!! (Oops—there's that hate, again.)

## Deeds

If you think of the game as steak being served up on a nice plate just for you, the words are the fat and the deeds are the meat. Unfortunately, once you've carved away the fat, most times you're left with something your dog would laugh at. Baby would rather have a Snausage (and maybe, come to think of it, so should you).

The deeds are the tangible efforts of the game. They can be broken down into two categories: Things and Time. Things include the money, gifts, jewelry, et cetera, that some players willingly and easily give. They also include the fixing of the sink, the changing of the tire, the loaning of the car, and other meaningful services provided by the player. Time encompasses the walks in the park, the accompaniment to the movies, Thanksgiving dinner with your family, visits while you're sick, et cetera. Sometimes you cannot easily separate the things and the time. There is often an overlap. If the player takes you on vacation, or out to dinner (that he, not you, pays for), then he's giving you both things *and* time. And believe me, he definitely sees it that way. So keep this in mind when you take him on a trip around the world at your expense and he doesn't seem grateful in the least bit upon your return. He did give you his time, didn't he? Remember, everything the player gives, *whatever* it is, is platinum. Your paying for the trip just doesn't equal the value of his precious time to accompany you on the trip.

The overlap of things and time needs to be examined closely. More often than not, the player gives the double-doobie. As mentioned above, the dinners and vacations paid for are both. So are the small things, like taking you to the movies or bringing you some McDonald's. Those flowers he brings along on the 3:00 A.M. booty call are also credited to both the things and time score sheets. Matter of fact, the booty call *itself* is both. The time he spends to give you "The Big Thing" is the mother of all the double-doobies. Why do you think that as the game progresses the booty call comes without much notice, fanfare, or wrapping? It usually ends up being the only deed given (and even then, it's given sparingly) by that stage of the game. Everything else? That's right, you got it: just words.

The value of the deed is determined by the player and what he has at his disposal. We tend to value the deed by what effect it has on us. But if the true spirit of the gift is in the giving, then the true value of the deed is in the doing, not the receiving. (That was a very important point—you should read it again.) The true value of gift X is greater from the player who does not have gift X readily available than it is from the player who has it at his disposal. The player who travels a lot, and thus has many frequent-flyer miles, may fly you somewhere for a romantic weekend. While it appears to be a big deal, it's actually a small part of what he has access to. But the player without funds who manages to take you on an overnight trip to Atlantic City is throwing his "A" game your way. Still game—just different levels of game from different players. And the level of the game played is determined by the value of the deed to the player.

If a player is willing to be viewed as doting on someone in public, on his playing field, regardless of who's on the field or who witnesses him on the field, over a significant period of time, then he's bringing out his "A" game. Nothing is confused with sincerity more than the player's "A" game. The "A" game is full of that player's best words and best deeds. Spending New Year's Eve with a player is "A" game. Going to a wedding of a player's family member—"A" game. Getting a key to a player's apartment—stupid, yes, but "A" game nonetheless. It doesn't have to be good game to be "A" game—it's just that particular player's best moves, whatever that player values most. If a player is an auto mechanic and seems to not mind helping friends and family with their cars, then the tune-up he gave you, even though your car desperately needed it, was not of much value to him. But if he was the kind of player who charges his destitute little sister for an oil change, then you know that he puts a high value on his work and doesn't give it away easily. Your free tune-up was part of his "A" game.

Sometimes the deeds are obscure. I know a player—a player's player—whose major pulling card is his ability to dance. Boy, that man can move. Now you might not think that dancing would be enough, but honey-chile, let me tell you. Until someone's swept you off your feet and made you feel like you're Ginger Rogers, you can't know how good it feels. (Yes, Fred Astaire was not fine. But that man was cool and sexy in his own right—the women adored him and the men honored him.) Now this dancing player would come in a room and dance with almost everyone. But when he came back to you a second time, you knew you were special. And when he danced with you three or four times in one night, he might as well have sent you candy and roses. You were on your way to being hooked. His only interaction with you might have been just a few phone calls and the promise of some good dancing when you ran into him again at the club. Unless he blessed you with some nookie (yeah, that was his other major deed) this was the extent of his interaction with you. And that was okay, 'cause whatever it was, it felt good. So when he pulls his "A" game out, he'll show it by dancing with you almost exclusively. Again, might not seem like much game, but trust—it was and it still is.

Sometimes the deeds are overt. I know a player who would cook for you, wash your car, paint your house, hell, even darn your socks. He is knowledgeable and willing to share his knowledge with you. He'll take you to nice places and buy you nice things. He is dependable, reliable, and consistent. This player's deeds are all right in your face, so much so that he appears to be just a nice guy looking for someone who he can treat nice. HAH! Just game. Turns out that how much he does depends on what level of game he is playing at any particular time, on any particular mark.

## Levels of the Game
You may need to know a player better to recognize the level of the game he is playing. It may appear that those phone calls from the player who talks to you

all night long are indicative of his true desire for you. But when you get to know him, you'll begin to notice that his phone begins to ring off the hook every night about 9:00 or so. These are calls from women who know he likes to talk and are trying to be the one he talks to tonight. What have you learned? He's just a phone person. Talking all night long is just what he does. Women love it and it's an easy and comfortable thing for him to do. No real effort on his part is required. Game yes, but "A" game, no.

Knowing the level of the game being played is quite helpful in determining how to respond. Not responding to his old, tired, worn-out game may force a better game from the player. After all, the player doesn't pull out his best every time he plays. Most of the marks he attains are with his "B" to "C" level game. At some point, the player knows what is usual and customary for him and he gravitates toward that type of mark with his standard game. He is most comfortable at this level and does not mind repeating this level of game over and over. The level of risk is low and the return is bountiful and, usually, guaranteed.

However, though it means moving out of his comfort zone, most players are always on the lookout for a mark who is not so accessible and available, who will force him to dig deep into his bag of tricks. A mark who will force the player to bring out his "A" game. Attaining these marks proves once again that the player still has what it takes.

## Two ‖ The Game in Play

AT THIS TIME, I wish to acknowledge that even though I have denominated the player as "he" and the mark as "she," I am well aware of the many female players that are out there successfully playing the game. I personally feel we women are actually better built to be players. And most male players will admit that female players play the game extremely well, even better than their male counterparts. However, for the sake of simplicity (it's quite a daunting task to start every phrase with "he or she"), I will address the player as "he" and the mark as "she." But I am in no way slighting the female players, or "playettes" as they are sometimes referred to. Mad props to the sistas! You go, girls!

In this chapter, I'd like to discuss the game as it is played. First and foremost, realize that there is no one way to play the game. The game is as varied and diverse as the ensembles at "The Players Ball." Yet there are basic patterns to the game that have remained the same. Ask an old player who has played and watched the game for fifty years, and he'll tell you that the young bucks ain't doing nothing different. Ask a young player and he'll tell you that the game is far more advanced now then it ever was. He'll talk about technology and its effect on the game. He'll talk about the new player being slicker and the new marks being more plentiful and more amenable to the game. He'll talk about the shortage of brothers that ultimately forces marks into the arms of players. But check back with him in fifteen years and he too will say the game's pretty much the same. There are three basic stages of the game: The Baiting Stage, Running Game, and The Finished Line (not Finish, Finished—the line or point by which the player has pretty much accomplished what he wants to accomplish and is for all intents and purposes finished).

**The Baiting Stage**
Herein the player meets a mark. While the player may meet many potential marks, what really determines who the mark will be is often nothing more than the player's personal preference at that particular time. A player looks at most if not all women as potential marks, so it's up to him to decide whom he will play with.

As soon as the initial contact is made, the game begins. To the unsuspecting mark, it may seem that they are both jockeying for position. Who initiates the phone calls? Who asks whom out on dates? Who is perceived as chasing whom? But what's really happening is the player is deciding how to bait the mark. What is the right bait and the right amount of bait required for the mark to bite? Plainly put, what does the player need to do to ensure that the mark is interested enough to involve herself with the player? As the player advances on the mark, it may appear to the mark that she is holding the cards. She might think, "I'm in control. If I want this or that, I'll do this or that. If I don't like what is going on I can stop, because I'm in control." Actually, the mark is in control at this point—at least, more in control than she will be at any other point in the game, because she is still in control of her emotions and can easily walk away. However, the player is not concerned with being in control at this point in the game. His game is just starting and he's looking at the big picture. He knows he will win and win big in the end. So he'll let the mark have the perceived control for now. The player is systematically baiting the mark.

## Running Game

The game begins with the words. They may be many or few, boisterous or meek, slick or sincere. Some players don't do much talking, but their few utterances are carefully designed to get your attention. These words are a pivotal part of the player's repertoire and have been tested over and over again. They are designed to send you home thinking about what he said. Something for you to take back to the girls. "Chile, I met this guy and let me tell you what he said. It was deep."

Deep indeed. It's the player's business to be "deep." More often than not, the mark can recite almost verbatim those opening lines from the player, even years later. That's how deep and memorable they are. But if you ever held a meeting of the marks of a particular player, you'd find that those memorable lines were used on all of them.

The deeds are actually few at first, but will more than likely soon escalate. Again, how much the player is actually willing to do is determined by the level of game he is playing, and the level of the game the player plays is contingent upon how much he wants that mark, for whatever reasons, and how resistant that mark is to the current level of game being played. For example, the mark might be exceptionally beautiful, or have a great body or some other glowing physical attribute. The mark might be the popular girl, or the new girl on the scene that everyone wants. In my experience, the mother of all marks seems to be the ex-queen of a known player. *Mrs. Player*: the one who has actually captured a player, but for whatever reasons is no longer with him. This is the mark who a player wanted to grow old with, the one that he would have stayed with if she could have just hung in there until his game ran out. But she couldn't. So when she's back on the market, a lot of other players are tempted to dust off their "A" game and try it on her. While this might be a dangerous move for a player, as the ex-queen knows a thing or two about the game, it is too intriguing to pass up. This queened mark represents that which has already been deemed worthy by a member of the player brotherhood. As such, other players want to prove that they can mark that queen, too. (What usually happens is the next player winds up trying to queen her as well—we'll talk later about how a mark gets queened.)

The mark herself is the biggest factor in determining the player's game. What the mark says, what the mark does, how the mark responds—these factors determine what moves the player will make. In the beginning of the game, when his desire level is highest, the player is inspired to do much more of what is necessary to get her. However, the mark usually spends a lot of time unwittingly providing the player with the ammunition that will cause her doom. For example, women tend to talk about their past relationships. What the relationship was like, what the person did wrong (mostly wrong—we tend to forget the right while remembering the wrong in great detail), why and how it ended. I believe women do this so that they can walk into new relationships clear of blame, excusing their failures at the door: "There's nothing wrong with me. It wasn't my fault. He did this, this, and this. And I couldn't take it any longer, so I left." Or, "He did this, this, this, and this and then he left, and I'm glad he's gone." Either way, when a player hears that this, this, and this worked on the mark, he's pretty much apt to try this, this, and this. Worked before and, if packaged a little differently, might work again. If not, oh well, something else in his arsenal will.

So the player will come at the mark with his game, and here at the outset, the mark might even know for a fact that it is game. The mark might even announce to the player, her girlfriends, and anyone else who happens to be listening, "This is game and I'm not falling for it." But what does the true player do? He tightens his game up a little and continues right on the same track. He knows that the mark will eventually fall for the game. All he has to do is be persistent. Persistence beats resistance.

Soon the pace quickens. At this point, the player is spending more time with the mark. He's charming her with those soft, sexy lines that are guaranteed to make her feel all gushy inside. He's calling all the time, quoting love songs. He needs to be with the mark more and more. Now the mark is in heaven. The player—who appeared to be just another player at the outset—now feels like a man who just needs some love, and who is truly willing to give some love in return. He's just been waiting for *you*. Most of the deeds the player will do will be done at this early stage of the game. The walks in the park. The accompanying you to the store while you shop, just to be with you. The weekend trips (remember, just because he pays doesn't mean it's not game, ladies).

What is the mark thinking? This feels like LOVE, the love that's described in all those self-help books. The kind you're supposed to be looking for. This is the game (for this particular mark) at its max. So take a picture, 'cause it's not gonna last. If ever there was a time for the mark to maintain the resistance, to stay aloof, to protect herself and stay in control, this is the time. But mark that you are, you don't.

### The Finished Line

Time goes on. The mark gradually begins to realize that even though she's open, receptive, and available to the player, he isn't nearly as open, receptive, and available to her. He's begun to distance himself. The deeds, whether things or time, are dwindling in frequency. He doesn't return her calls, and if he does he takes his time about it. He's not willing to listen to her complain or voice her displeasure with the current state of affairs. The mark's best attempts at making plans or getting him to commit to doing anything at all with her are in vain. Even if the mark says she's done with him, he does little to dissuade her. And if he does, then it's only to keep the mark in standby mode. Even though the player won't admit it to the mark (not if she asks, or begs, or pleads for him to be truthful with her), the player is pretty much "finished." He's accomplished what he set out to do, and his interests are probably directed toward the new mark of the day.

## The Gardeners—An Analogy

By now you must have realized that I am the Analogy Queen, the "let me put it to you this way" master. Oh well, that's my style. Anyway, let's look at the relationship between the player and the mark as starting out like two yards on opposite sides of a fence. You're in your garden, he's in his, and the gate is closed. But eventually you meet. You notice, and he is quick to make sure you notice, that this man glows like the sun! After a while you and he begin to lean over the fence and play, but you're still in your yard, still tending to your life, your garden. He begins to lean on the gate, making sure that his glow is shining in your garden. Your garden is warming up quite nicely now due to his effervescent glow. But you still think it best that you keep the gate closed. But he keeps leaning and leaning and things are getting so nice and warm in your garden.

Eventually the player leans on your gate until you open it up, just a bit, for all of his goodness and light to come in. The player sets one foot into your yard. Immediately, his presence, his glow, has lit up your entire garden. The glow has made your flowers grow taller, your roses bloom, your daffodils daff. You believe that this is what you've been looking for. This is real. And so is he! And so you think, "Let me welcome that glow with openness and receptiveness. 'Cause I want him to know I like what I'm feeling." So you take a giant step toward him. He, for his part, stands his ground. He may even move a little closer. But he doesn't move too far away from that gate.

Now everything's blooming. Everything's growing. This is how your garden should and could be. The player's watering this, he's nurturing that, he's on the verge of coming all up in your garden. Now it's time for you to open up completely, so that he'll know that you're deserving of his warmth. So you open up. Wide. You let go of any reserve you had. You're his, and you're ready to embrace whatever he has to give. But the player's still basically at the gate. The gate's still open, and he really hasn't advanced far from it. Suddenly, and without much fanfare, he shifts his weight, and it sort of looks like he's kind of leaning toward the gate, toward his garden and away from yours. It's obvious that he cares. He showed the warmth of his feelings when he was watering and nurturing your garden, didn't he? But he might not be ready to move completely into your garden. He shares more with you: that he has reservations. That some women are dogs, too. That he could get hurt. That he's been hurt before.

So now you think that maybe something you said or did wasn't quite right, that you sent him the wrong message. Maybe he's feeling that this isn't quite what he thought it was because you're acting a little different (are you, really?). Maybe things should slow down a bit. So he backs away a little. Okay. So you come a little closer toward him. "Things are good, don't back away, we're gonna be fine, you can trust me," you say. But he backs away a little further. Now he's no longer in your yard. He's in his. Your yard is not quite as warm as it was when he was there.

There's still sunshine coming in because the gate is open and he still radiates. Your daffs are still daffing, your roses are still blooming, But things aren't looking nearly as bright as they were when he was inside the gate and you were close to him. So you move still closer. And he moves still further back. Now he's deep in his yard and you're between your safe ground, your yard, and his world.

You're feeling a little desperate now. He's not doing much of anything for your garden anymore because he's too far away. But you're still reaching toward him; it feels warmer when you're closer to him. (Even if the only thing being warmed is you and not your garden.) So you leave your garden and now you're in his. There's no sun at all in your yard. You're not there to water it, you're not there to nurture it. Your garden's going to pot. What do you do? You begin to water his garden, make his garden better, hoping he will see how nice it can be with you there in his garden (not him in yours—you've left yours behind, remember). Maybe you and he can garden together in his garden. And maybe, eventually you can knock down the fence between your yard and his and have this one big beautiful garden.

But does he work with you? No, he goes into his house. So you stop gardening. You're not gonna tend his garden by yourself, even if you're trying to do it for the both of you. Then he comes back out and says, "I was just about to come out and help. Look, here's a nice glass of wine and some cheese to snack on. But if you don't want to do any work with me, I understand." No, that's not the case. Of course you want to garden with him. He's still being nice, and he even brought you that wine, didn't he? Might have even raked a leaf or two with you. Gave you a nice massage and made you feel good again. So you decide to hang in there and keep on taking care of his garden. And guess what he does—he lets you. And he goes back into his house. Now, you're really gonna step it up a notch. When he does come back out, he's gonna find out that you're the best damn gardener in the whole damn world. But what happens when he does come back out? He brings you a glass of soda, hangs around for a minute, maybe rubs your back a little, then it's back into the house.

At this point, the player has you. You're in his world. Left yours behind. And your garden has gone to weed. You keep trying to keep his garden nice for him, just the way he wants it, so that when he comes back out and looks at it, he'll just want to keep you in his garden. But when he shows up again—and he will show up—he barely has a lukewarm glass of water for you. If you dare mention the fact that he never comes out into the garden with you, he accuses you of complaining too much, and he goes back inside. Next time he comes out, you don't even complain for fear he'll hightail it back in. But he hightails it back in anyway. If you look like you're going to turn and go out of the gate, he comes out and puts forth just enough effort to stop you. Because he doesn't want to let you go. He didn't do all of that to let you go. He wants you to keep things tidy and nice in his garden.

One day, as you're looking around, you notice that there is another garden on the other side of the player's house. And there's another gardener in it with a glass of lukewarm water just working away. And as you continue to look around you spot yet another garden. And there at that gate is the player, leaning over and vigorously watering someone else's garden.

That's the game.

In the beginning things were going very well for you. You were relatively happy and you were sure that this relationship was moving forward. But at some point, things took a turn for the worst. Somewhere along the line, you gave up all of yourself for a chance at a real relationship. But what you got was

### *PLAYED!!*

# Three  ‖  A Closer Look at the Player

WHAT MAKES A PLAYER A PLAYER? Is it his good looks, his chiseled body, his wit, his charm? Is he clean from head to toe? Do the girls all pause when he walks into the room?

Maybe. But then again, maybe not. Some players project so much energy that it does feel as if the room has stopped moving when they walk in. You can almost feel their heat when your back is turned on them. They radiate a confidence that beams like a beacon, shining down on the unsuspecting but all too willing prey. It can't be mistaken for anything else. You only have that kind of confidence when you know you have what they all want. When you know that you are just that damn good. A quick sultry glance from those eyes, a slight nod of that head on that magnificent body, a little hint of a smile from those lips, and BAM! You've been marked. To the player, the rest is history.

But players come in all forms and fashions. That quiet guy who comes into the club and barely speaks to you week after week could very well be the biggest player in the room. You may never really see him coupled with anyone, or you may only notice him engaged in some light conversation. But if you take a closer look, you'll see that he may be on the quiet side, but he's quietly very confident, too. You'll observe that other women genuinely enjoy talking to him. He doesn't put himself out there for you to notice, but you'll find yourself talking with him about the weather, some current event, or (and this is a classic player move) what upcoming functions you might be attending. Oh yes—he will coincidentally show up at that same function. This keeps happening and before you know it, BAM! You've been marked.

Let's compare these two types of players further. You're out at the club (I like to use the club scenario, but please believe me, the same mode of player operation can be used anywhere: the laundromat, the supermarket, your child's school, church…). Let's call Mr. Out There In Your Face "Player A." He comes right at you, staring at you like you're a Reese's Peanut Butter Cup that he's about to eat up, with some slick greeting, like "Waz up baby" or "Hey sweetness."

Now "Player B," Mr. Oh I'm Such a Nice Quiet Guy, he comes by and says, "Hi, how are you doing? Good to see you again." Player A might start flexing and strutting his stuff all over the room, just so you can get a preview of the coming attraction. Player B may engage in some light conversation with someone else in the room or go stand off by himself.

Both players will make their way back to you at least two more times before they leave the club. (This is the "three contact rule," another way you know you're being marked; trust me, this is just something I know.) At some point, some contact info is exchanged. This may not happen immediately, as players don't necessarily rush the onset of the game unless there's a reason. Player A might just drop his card on you and tell you to give him a call. He's confident that you can recognize a good thing when you see it and that you will follow up. And if not, well, that's your loss. Player B may come up with a reason why the two of you should have some additional contact outside of the current arena. He may have some pictures for you from a party, or a gift from the past holiday that he'd like to give to you, or maybe some information or help with a problem that you might have, based on a previous conversation between the two of you. Or he might just invite you out for a cup of coffee. Whatever the situation calls for, the player will find a way to ensure that you want to contact him.

While Player A and Player B employ different methods, they're all means to the same end. Once they've established a method of contact, then you'd better believe the game is on. From that point forward, the game is being played under the basic strategy of the player baiting the mark with deeds and words, ultimately reducing his output of deeds, and eventually words, while not affecting his input from the mark.

A note: both types of players will allow you to delude yourself into believing that what the two of you share is more than it actually is. However, when Player A is involved, this can't really be more than a shallow delusion. With Player A, you absolutely know that this is game. You know what drum he was drumming when you saw him walking around banging on it. If you convince yourself that the melodious sound of the violin was amazingly pouring out of his drum, that's your delusion. When he walks away still banging on that drum, which incidentally now sounds exactly like a drum, don't be surprised.

Now Player B, on the other hand, well, he's not too obvious—or honest—with his game. He will use the nice guy thing to the max. He walks up to you, violin in hand, playing a cute little ditty on it. As you get a little closer to him, he hits you with the rhapsodies and concertos and you think, "Wow—this is just the music that I've been looking for!" Then, all of a sudden, he pulls out the drum and walks away banging on it. Now, even though he misled you into believing the delusion, you still fell for it. The reality of who he was and what he was doing never changed. It was just revealed a bit more slowly.

Both players came at the mark. Both players relied on the mark letting them in. Both players used the mark's willingness to believe in the delusion against her. That is the Player's weapon. That is who the Player is.

Simply put:

**The player is he who uses another person's faith and trust in him to get what he wants.**

The player takes advantage of the mark's willingness to believe that *this* guy, regardless of what you know or don't know about him, is sincerely interested in engaging in a meaningful relationship. A player relies on the fact that you will put an "and, therefore…" at the end of every little sweet, sexy, funny, or cute (albeit inconsequential) thing he does. "He stayed up and called me at 12:10 A.M. on Valentine's Day, just so he could say Happy Valentine's Day before he went to sleep. *And, therefore*, he must really care about me." Yeah, right! He probably called someone else at 12:15 with the same message.

A player once told me, "When I come up with a good line, I call them all and spread the sunshine around. It's amazing how much ground you can cover and how many gifts you can recover with just one good line."

This may seem cold. Well, the player is cold. He has to be to play the game. He can't afford to be persuaded by your displays of emotion. He really can't care about how his actions affect you. The game, at bottom, is about him, his conquest, his triumphs.

Think of it this way: the player does not view the mark as anything more than another mark—maybe with more skills, but a mark nonetheless and capable of being conquered. Keep in mind that to the player, what is at stake is a *win*, a conquest. The player cannot lose—he can only *not win*. The game will work or not. He'll either conquer the mark or not. He doesn't lose anything because he doesn't stake anything. He knows he has to pay some cost—some words, some time, some things—to play the game. But whatever he dishes out is pretty much what he had planned to dish out at the onset.

### Why Does the Player Play?

In the process of writing this book, I've shared bits and pieces of it with some of my friends as well as some acquaintances who happened by while I was in the midst of writing. (I wrote everywhere: on the train, while in meetings, watching TV, while getting my hair done, even while out at the club.) The question that I'm always asked is, "Why does the player play?"

Because he can. The truth of the matter is, he plays because he's allowed to. It has become a sport and he's learned to win. The benefits of playing the game are many. And while there may be many reasons not to play the game (like true love or the ever-elusive conscience), the game is just too attractive.

Some people tend to think that the player is substituting the conquest of women for something else that he is unable to conquer. Some think that the game promotes and sustains a big fat inflated ego. Others tend to believe that the player is in it for the ease and variety of the gifts and pleasures obtained from the mark. Still others think that the player has some deeply seated hatred or distrust for women—maybe because of a relationship gone badly or some residual mother issues that have led the player to seek out women to hurt. Another theory is that the player grew up with women catering to his every need, an adoring mother, grandmother, or maybe lots of sisters who took complete care of him. Thus, normal for him is when women are catering to him, and that's easier with lots of women. It is also possible that the player just may love women and love being surrounded by many of them. And let's not forget: the player just might like to have lots of sex with lots of women.

If you could examine the individual personal lives of a group of players, you would probably uncover most if not all of the issues and reasons cited above lurking inside them. An in-depth psychological profile of the player may uncover even more underlying problems. But since these are traits or life experiences that can't necessarily be changed (at least not within the confines of this book), and since I don't think that overanalyzing the inner psyche of the player will help the mark play the game any better, I'll leave the closer review of these issues to those better equipped to do it. I'm sure there's a book or two on the shelves already that will cover it, if you need to go any deeper. But this just ain't that kind of book.

## When and How Does a Player Start Playing?

"Baby, I was born a player and will die a player. And in between, I'm gonna PLAY."

It does seem that some players have been playing all of their lives. Like they jumped out the womb smack-dab into game, macking girls in the hospital nursery. That may be a bit absurd, but some players do get started awful early.

I know one young boy who's just pretty. Too pretty to be a boy, and much too pretty for his own good. He's about thirteen and started playing girls about a year ago. Now, since twelve-year-old girls aren't normally giving up what a player wants (whatever that is), you can bet that he is playing with some older girls. Girls as old as eighteen are chasing this boy's butt down. Don't ask me what they want from this little boy, 'cause the child don't stand no higher than five feet tall, but chase him they do. And if you think twelve was too early to start, consider that if that boy had gotten the height gene, he might have been macking at nine or ten!

Earlier we talked about that certain something that players have that makes them attractive to others. Men usually find out that they possess that certain something after they've already begun to use it. The young player-in-the-making may not have found someone who knocks him off his feet, and if he has, he probably hasn't mustered up the courage to approach her. But the girls all hang around him. Someone always has notes for the class he missed. Someone's always volunteering to watch his books when he's playing ball. Someone's always eager to share whatever they're munchin' on with him (and he's always taking from them, even if he doesn't know it yet). Does this make him a player? No, it just makes him attractive, and there's nothing's wrong with that. Does it make him predisposed to being a player? Maybe, but not necessarily. It just means that he may have the tools, should he lean towards a player's lifestyle. This attractive youngster may fall in love. He could get into a serious monogamous relationship and stay there. Let's say that happens. Even though he's taken, his attractiveness draws other women to him. But he's devoted and he remains faithful, never venturing too far outside of love's boundaries. Here he may live happily ever after till death they do part. It *could* happen!

Here's another scenario. Same youngster falls in love, gets into a serious relationship and stays there for about a decade or so. Something happens, they grow apart, and he finds himself out of the relationship. (He may be still in it, but emotionally he's out—it's the same difference.) He's an attractive man and the women are drawn to him. He's been out of the dating game, so he's not very smooth or skilled. But it doesn't seem to matter. He begins to get more and more rhythm for his efforts. So he reduces his output and, lo and behold, the response is that he continues to receive rhythm. This works for him and it's easy. So he continues. He's in the game.

Let's look at it from yet another perspective. Same

attractive youngster, he kinda likes this girl, but she doesn't like him. But a lot of others do. And the girls are being so nice to him. And he gets used to it. Now, when one of them is not happy because he's not doing this thing or that thing, he's not pressured to make any real changes, because there's another one standing by who is willing to accept him no matter what he does. And it's much easier to switch to another one then to attempt to soothe the hurt one. Soon he begins to expect that women will be amenable to him and his actions, and when they're not— SWITCH! He is now playing the game. He's taking and taking and moving on, giving little or nothing in return.

In each case the guy was attractive as a youth and in each case his attractiveness provided him with the opportunity to be a player. In scenario #1, he found love and pretty much lived there. Even though he could have been a player, and may even have strayed a time or two (or was, at the very least, tempted), for the most part he stayed within the boundaries of his relationship. This is not fantasy, folks. This can and does happen in real life. It may be rare, but it happens often enough that we can still have hope that it will happen to us. (Keep hope alive! But don't hold your breath, ladies.)

In scenario #2, he was in a relationship for a long time, but once out, found playing the game to be fruitful and relatively easy for him. The game offered him the benefits that come with being in relationships, but without the emotional attachment. And he is probably in no hurry to get back to that type of attachment.

Scenario #3 finds the young man never having been in a meaningful relationship before the lure of the game pulls him into its grasp. He has learned the art of the game at an early age and will continue to play it until some life-altering event happens. This doesn't mean that a real relationship isn't in the cards for this player. It just means that it didn't precede his getting into the game. He may yet find himself in a real one-on-one relationship. Or he may play until he dies or is too old to receive the fancy of any more women. (Though even then he'll probably have a woman or two in the bank, so don't feel bad for the old player.)

Not all players have those drop-dead good looks. Conversely, and luckily for us, not all fine brothers are players! Plenty of players are average-looking guys, but these guys may have been (or are) very popular, and thus very attractive, because of what they could do or what they possessed. The athletes, the musicians, the children of the rich and famous, all find themselves irresistible to the opposite sex and therefore suitable candidates for the player lifestyle, if they so choose. What's interesting to note, though, is that even if later on they are no longer athletes or musicians or blessed with riches and fame, the confidence they developed keeps them player-eligible.

OK, so how about the average Joe? What makes him so attractive that he is able to assume the role of a player? It's his confidence. That is the common denominator among all players. All the average Joe has to do is to *know* (not think) that he is desirable. Now, what makes women desire him? What draws them to him? Could be the way he dresses, or talks, or walks, or smiles. Could be that he has a particular skill or quality that is in demand—not necessarily sex, but we definitely can't rule that out. If looks or talent or fame or money or good sex or even (fake) sensitivity is what women want, then the guy who has it is the guy women want. And once he *knows* he's wanted, he has the kind of confidence that comes with knowing that women will tolerate whatever he does or doesn't do because they want him. He knows that when one finally gets tired of his game and stops playing with him, another one is waiting to start.

## The Player Develops His Game

Regardless of how or when a player gets into the game, once in, he's almost always hooked. He relishes the opportunity to play each new mark he fancies. He begins to hone his skills as if he were a prizefighter training for a title shot, polishing and shaping his game until it is uniquely his. Different from every other player! Best game on the block!

It starts out with the desire for the most basic reward of all: the reward of sex. Even seasoned players will tell you that sexual attraction is generally the fundamental motivating factor that drives a player to a mark. The conquest of fresh meat reaffirms the player's ability to play. Even when time takes over and the player isn't what he used to be sexually, he generally finds enough energy (or Viagra) to get it up for new meat. When a retired player is asked why he quit the game, the standard answer seems to be, "Man, I was just getting old and needed to settle down." But what he probably means is "Man, the wang is getting old and just don't respond like it used to."

With sex as the primary goal, a man might begin to move from woman to woman, getting all he can. Since he's only one man, he begins to prioritize his women, with the best or most sexually engaging of the lot getting the most attention. Soon, most or all of these women become old news, and he opens his doors to fresh meat. Now he's becoming a player. Now he's on the hunt for women, knowing damn well he doesn't want a relationship—he's just looking to play.

So the new player throws out his hook. Now, he's new to the game—he's got a little hook and not the best bait on it. But because he's desirable, women bite. Maybe not all of the women, or the type of women whom he'd most like to bite, but he does get a bite or two, and that's enough at this stage of his development. He adds them to his collection.

Whatever his game is, this is basically how it goes. As all players do, he starts out strong, attentive, interested. Whatever deeds he's gonna do, he's gonna do them with these new marks. Whatever picture he's gonna paint of what the relationship between him and the mark will be, this is when he paints it. The word game is in full effect. This is when he hooks the mark. Again, as with all players, his game will work or not work. The player will win or not win. (Remember, he doesn't lose, he either wins or not.) If they fall for it, then they're hooked. When they're hooked, the player will enjoy them as he wants to enjoy them until the newness wears off. Since he's already won, he can afford to level his game off to a comfortable pace, giving himself some time to devote to his other marks that have been reduced to standby mode.

But what of the player's old standby marks? He's busy cultivating the new ones and doesn't have as much time as he used to for them. He stops calling them and stops answering their calls. The standby marks only receive enough game to keep them on hold. Many marks walk out of the game after spending time on standby. There are generally not enough words, not to mention deeds, to keep those marks hopeful that the player will play with them again.

But even if the player is done with these old marks, they won't hear it from him. He is not likely to dismiss them permanently. After all, he never knows when he may need to run up on it again. So even if the mark does leave, it still doesn't mean the player's charms won't work on her anymore. He may run into her again, and since *he* never dismissed *her*, he'll point out that *she* left *him*. When she asks, "Why did you stop calling me?" he answers with a vague comment like, "I didn't stop calling you, you stopped calling me," or "Something was going on and I had to get myself together, and when I turned around, you were gone." But never does he admit to dumping her. And never does he ask her to come back. If he wants to get back with her, he usually will—but only for as far and as long as he wants. Then he'll back away from her just like he did before and turn his attention elsewhere.

Sadly, some marks get into the standby mode and stay there indefinitely. Most players will have at least one or two "lifers" who have stood the test of time and will be there whenever the player calls. Seems these marks always think that the player will tire and retire, and then will reward their diligence with a "forever" relationship. Not likely to happen. Think about it. You don't keep your old coat around because you think it will become your everyday coat again. You keep it around because you haven't thrown it away yet. But when you are forced to clean out your closet, for whatever reason, the old coat goes.

The player never worries that the supply of marks will dry up. He assumes that he will always be able to have more than one woman. I once heard a player's mother say about her son, "Them women ain't gonna want him when he gets old. Them women ain't gonna be chasing him like they've been doing. Then he'll be in trouble." This is not something that the player himself thinks, however. If he gets out of the game, it won't be because the market has completely dried up. It'll be because for whatever reasons, he's decided that he doesn't want to play anymore.

The player continues this cycle of baiting potential marks, acquiring them, having his way with them, and then reducing them to standby mode. As the new player develops, so does the quality of his game. And thus, the goals of the particular player's game begin to reflect more of who he is. Some players only want sex. That's it. When, where, and how they get it may change, may become more intriguing or even outlandish. However, most players want something more from their marks. Some players want women who buy them things, take them on trips, or furnish their homes. Some players need women to help them in this or that aspect of their business. Some players need to be seen with a different pretty and obedient woman on their hip at all times. Some want housemaids or cooks. Some just want money. Some may not know what they want—but they know, whatever it is, they want it to be given to them by women.

Once in, the player goes about the business of incorporating the game into his everyday life. Being on the lookout for potential marks is intrinsic to everything he does. All women not related to him are henceforth categorized by whether or not they are of mark quality. He has no qualms about how he thinks of or what he does to the marks. He is the goodness, and he bestows himself upon them. By his reckoning, the marks are, in fact, lucky.

As he becomes more skilled, the player reduces what he gives—the deeds, whether things or time—to very little. He is able to ration out minimal portions to the marks, always keeping the bulk of himself to himself. The benefits to him? By giving very little to any particular mark, he is able to service a larger pool of potential, existing, and standby marks. There is always room for more marks in the stable. And he is always in a position to substantially increase what he needs to give if a situation calls for it.

## The Player's Rules

Ha! As if they really have any. (Was that just hate? Oops. Sorry. Again.)

While there is no player code of ethics, a player does well to keep in mind certain key elements of the game. I think that every player would tell you that the cardinal rule of the game is "Don't hate." To be more specific: don't be jealous or resentful or begrudge a player his successes. Don't delight in his failures. Don't interfere in another player's game in any way, shape, or form. In particular, don't inject into a player's game any information, advice, et cetera, that would jeopardize said player's game and, thus, its outcome. The marks of the world do not need to hear *anything* about a player, or the game, from another player. The player is better off when the mark is ignorant of the game. (Oh my goodness—is this book breaking the cardinal rule? Why hell yeah!)

Now, this doesn't mean that a player can't mark another player's mark. Oh no. A mark is fair game. A good player will tell you that the mark is free to see whomever she wants to see. What that really means is that if the player is really working his game, the mark will not *want* to see anyone else. So another player making advances toward the mark will not have any impact. If by chance a mark goes for another player's game, then so be it. There is no reason for the player to resent the other player. It's competitive sport: the best game wins. Simple as that.

The next major rule? Don't play a player. His entire game is thrown off when he encounters another player. The playing field has been leveled by the other player's ability to respond strategically to the player's actions and not get caught up by emotions. The player can get played. The stakes are now win or *lose*, not win or not-win. Now while the idea of playing the game against another player might sound like the sport of kings, most players find the risk is generally too high. Why?

1. Someone will get played. And let me tell you, almost the saddest thing you will ever see is a played player. I say almost, because nothing, but nothing, is sadder than a player who

got caught up and fell in love, and love left him. (We'll talk about love and the player a little later—promise.)

2. The player who wins the game against another player now has a disgruntled player on his hands, who most likely knows she's been played and can't wait for revenge. The player who won may only have won Round One. Round Two might kick his butt. Again, too risky.

3. The game played has to involve much more in the way of tangible deeds, as the other player is well aware of the word game and ain't having it. All in all, playing a player is a whole 'nother game. And while undeniably exciting, there are many losses on both sides and probably not much pure profit other than bragging rights.

## The Player's Preferences and Obstacles

The player views most women as merchandise in the mark supermarket. He picks and chooses which ones he wants to play with. Most players believe that given the right circumstances, all women are capable of being captured and played. When a player fails to attract a particular mark, it's due solely to circumstances and not in any part to the player's inability to "get" her. What might these circumstances be? Perhaps a total and complete unwillingness to deal with men for a while. (We've all been there before, haven't we?) Or the potential mark might relocate to Siberia or something and be outside of the player's reach. Or the potential mark may be in love and happy. Take note: not just in love, and not just happy. A lot of players manage to slip in where love but not happiness lives. Also, since one of the player's talents is his ability to make the mark happy (when he wants to), he can make the happy mark even happier. But women tend not to stray from the combination of love and happiness.

The yang of this is that certain other circumstances beyond the player's control might enhance his probability of conquering the mark. Take, for example, the mark who is at the tail end of an unhappy, unfulfilling relationship. Easy prey for the player.

It seems that the player particularly likes marks who are one-man women. The monogamous mark puts everything she has to give into one person. There is no need for the player to compete for her affection and attention. Therefore, when the player is not feeding her the attention and affection she needs, she goes hungry. The player likes his marks hungry. That way, whatever crumbs he chooses to throw the mark's way, the mark is grateful for. (This is another reason why the player is reluctant to play another player. Nobody's hungry.)

Many players also like to keep at least one married mark in their stables. You might think that a married mark's obligations would prevent the player from obtaining much of anything from her. *Au contraire*! The married mark offers all the benefits without any of the liabilities. Consider:

- The married mark does not need the player to be the man in her life. She has a man.

- The deeds that the mark expects from the player are thus limited.
- The mark does not require a lot of time from the player. She herself doesn't have a lot of time to give.
- The married mark wants her attention and affection from the player in brief, high-quality episodes. This is right up the player's alley. Those Wham, Bam, Thank-You Ma'ams are exactly what the player is built to give.

Many players will keep a married mark on hand for years. Even should this mark get a divorce, odds are her status with the player would not change. But don't feel sorry for this mark, because she too is getting her needs met in this arrangement—which makes her a lot better off than other marks. Think about it. If a player spends a one night a month with each of his marks, and the married mark can only get away one night a month to be with the player, then the married mark is getting 100 percent of her needs met. Now it doesn't always work out that the player is available to the married mark as often as the married mark is available to the player. In fact, most players will make sure that they aren't. Gotta keep calling the shots, as it were. But the married mark does come closer to getting what she wants from the player then the monogamous mark. Some may even argue that this is not game. I tend to believe that just because the mark is happy doesn't mean it's not game. But it may change into a mutually satisfactory "relationship" (per the dictionary) where the mark recognizes and accepts the limits.

## The Player's Habitat

While I don't believe that there is such an animal as the typical player, I do believe that certain modus operandi tend to emerge more frequently than others. Like where players typically congregate. There is no more typical habitat for the player than that quintessential player supermarket: the club. The club is the breeding ground, training site, battle station, and retirement home for many players. The young ones come to learn game, the seasoned ones come to play game, and the old ones come to watch and teach and recollect.

Try going to a club purely to observe players in their natural habitat; it might prove a very informative and enlightening undertaking. You'd find players in groups swapping stories of conquest. You'd witness some young player's awkward attempts at new game, or some old player's attempts to breathe life into a tired game. You'd see a few smooth players successfully managing three or four marks at the same time without breaking a sweat. You'd hear some good lines—and some wack lines. And if you look closely, you're likely to see the seeds of heartbreak, as more than a few women there will end up being played.

## Player Q&A

*Question: Is the guy who decides he no longer likes the woman he's with and moves on to another a player?* Not necessarily. The question to ask is, what was his original intent? To conquer, or to seek out a relationship? Note that I don't mean he has to be looking for a wife. He may be, but he may only want someone to kick it with. Too often, we confuse "he don't like me no more" with "he was just running game on me." It's only game if, from the door, the only objective was to "get" her, not to keep her.

*Question: Are all men players?*
No. Being a man doesn't' make you a player. Also, having played the game doesn't make you a player.

How many of you can play Chopsticks on the piano? Come on, raise your hands. Lots of hands up right now. Of you with your hands raised, how many of you have had some form of piano lessons and can, on demand, play two or three rudimentary songs? Look at those hands drop—but there are probably a good many hands still raised. (I know you readers have talent—go'n with your bad selves!) Now of those remaining with their hands up, who of you can actually work those ivory keys and bring forth a melodious rapture that stirs the heart and soul? Only a few of you still have your hands raised high (and proud of it, no doubt—to you I say bravo!). You are pianists, people who have become proficient in the art of piano playing.

Such is the player. Many recreational players dibble and dabble in the game, successfully playing here and there. Some even manage to get a good run going before circumstances stop them in their tracks. But the true player is a virtuoso. He keeps a steady flow of marks coming and going while maintaining a base of standbys. He doesn't get apprehensive when those love holidays come 'cause he knows he can talk his way out of being there or buying anything. Conversely, his birthday is an opportunity to get bombarded with gifts from marks who are, unbeknownst to them all, jockeying for position.

Understand that being a player is not what he *does*. It's who he *is*. In order for a real player to stop playing the game, a serious event must occur, and then a metamorphosis must take place (which may be a very slow process). Or he grows too old to move and dies.

No, I take that back. I'm sure there is game in the afterlife.

*Question: Does a player love?*
Yes.

*Question: That's it, that's all you have to say about the player and love?*
Oh no. I have a whole chapter for that. Didn't you read the Table of Contents?

*Question: Have you ever been played, Ms. T.?*
Yes. But my story will be another book. And baby, it's a doozie!

*Question: I'm a grown woman. I can tell game when I see it, can't I?*
No, you can't.

There's no problem if he decides to take the high road: "Baby, I'm just looking to hit it and run. Can you handle that?" If not—if his game is covert—then he will appear to be just a nice guy sincerely interested in you. By the time you recognize that it's game, you've been hooked, and you can't get out without pain or, at the very least, some level of discomfort.

Until now.

Note: Ladies, please—just because I've taken apart your player, don't run out there and think you're ready to handle his game. Finish the book. Buy your girlfriends copies. Have them read it and talk about it. Don't give them *your* book—you'll need it to refer to later. Have group meetings to discuss it. Invite me to them. I'll come. Do whatever you need to do to get to the point where this will all sink in and become second nature.

*Question: But Ms. T., you make the mark sound so sad and pathetically out of control. The picture you paint is so very bleak. Maybe I should just give up on men and relationships and take up knitting. Is that what you think I should do?*
Sure, take up knitting if you'd like. Send me a sweater. That would be nice. And maybe a matching scarf. And while you're at it, knit yourself a nice cozy room that you can crawl up into and hide away in.

Or...........................

# Four ‖ OK—So What Do I Do About It?

...OR, YOU CAN DECIDE that you're gonna take control.

Yeah. Maybe it's time to take control.

So many women I talk to about the subject of players and the game are so high and mighty about not getting played, they think that the women who are played are stupid and foolish—that they *deserve* to have been played. I'm sure that even as you are reading this little book, you'll run into a few other women with the same opinion. They'll look over your shoulder as you're reading and say, "Hmm, not me. The man's mama ain't been born who can play me!" And if you've just been played yourself, you may be feeling some kinda way about that.

Well, let me respond. Y'all listening? Here it is. If you're a grown woman and you haven't been played, then one of four things has happened:

1. You've been fortunate enough to find a good man, or a string of good men, and they've either not wanted to or not chosen to play you. (Notice I said *they* did not want to play you. Not that *you* did not want to or couldn't get played. Huge difference.)
2. You've been fortunate to deal only with men who didn't have a clue how to run game on you.
3. You've been on Venus, and since men are from Mars, you haven't run into any—players or otherwise.
4. You're a player yourself, or at least innately

astute at playing the game, and you've played instead of getting played. (If this is the case, please give those unfortunate brothers whom you've left in your wake a copy of this book.)

I am not saying that every woman who gets involved with a player will get played every time. I am saying that if you have had a relationship with a man, and you found out he was a player, chances are you found out because he played you. He may have only gotten a short game going on you before you found out and got out of there without too much damage. Or he may have been able to play a full-fledged game, and you found yourself on standby. Either way, you got played. Then again, you may have caught a player when he was vulnerable and his game was in remission. Or he may not have had a chance to play you before the relationship ended. Or he may have been struck by lightning and has now repented.

So for you who have not been played, I say, congratulations. Buy a copy or two of this book and pass it along to your less fortunate sisters. You owe them that for rubbing your good fortune in their faces.

Now to the rest of us, let's talk about what to do.

## Emotional Control

The number one way to ensure that you don't get played is to control your emotions. Emotional indifference to the player is like a cross to the vampire.

This strategy is paramount to countering the player's game. But of all the strategic moves, controlling your emotions is the most difficult. It is our nature to love and care for others. We want to find our mate and shower him with kindness and affection. We want and need to give him love.

**DON'T!**
**DON'T!**
**DON'T!**
**DON'T!**
**DON'T!**

Let me reiterate. Don't! Don't give him love.

Don't lead with your heart. Keep your heart. If you have to give him something that's important to you, then give him your body instead. I know this contradicts everything we've been taught. So before you throw this book down and pick up your outraged pens, give me a chance to explain.

We learn at an early age that having sex outside of marriage is a sin. Right? Fall in love, get married, have children (sex). That's the order. Getting married is where love is supposed to evolve. Marriage is love. So if sex outside of marriage is a sin, then having sex outside of love is, at the very least, morally wrong. Therefore, if we have sex, then love must either precede it or follow on its heels.

But the player doesn't play by your or my ideals. He plays with what works. You operating according to your emotions is what works for him. In fact, in order for you to get caught up in the game, you *have* to have some feelings for him. That way, you will excuse what he does or doesn't do *because* you want to believe in him, *because* you care.

So don't care.

Keeping your emotions in check is like climbing in the ring with a cup and headgear on. It's like playing football with pads and helmet. Like swimming with a life vest. It prevents you from getting hurt too badly. By keeping your emotions in check you also, in turn, prevent yourself from going in too deeply. While this does protect you, it can have a slightly negative effect. Consider that swimmer with the life vest on. The vest keeps her afloat and protects her from drowning. But it also hampers her maneuverability by preventing her from going in too deep. And deep is where the action is. Deep is where the pretty and interesting fish swim.

Protecting yourself by holding on to your emotions prevents you from obtaining the full benefits of the relationship. You don't get that ultimate feel-good that only comes from being with and enjoying someone you truly care about. On a 1-10 scale, with 10 equal to "feeling great" and 1 equal to "totally devastated", you hover around the 4-6 zone. Safe, but no fireworks. But that's OK. There's nothing wrong with being safe. If the relationship endures, there will be more than enough time to throw aside the life vest and dive deep. But for now, starting out, keep yourself protected emotionally.

Deciding to be emotionally detached is one thing, but actually being able to stay emotionally detached is quite another. Say being with this player makes you feel happy. We respond to feeling happy by directing our thoughts toward love, because love is *supposed* to make you feel happy. Therefore, if you feel happy, then you should be falling in love.

But why can't we just respond to feeling happy by simply feeling happy? There is nothing wrong with enjoying the moment. Nothing wrong with enjoying the flowers that he sent you. But there *is* something wrong with falling in love *because* he sent them to you. There's nothing wrong with appreciating the work he did on your house. There is, however, something wrong with falling in love with him because he did it. And finally: There's nothing's wrong with enjoying that amazing sexual interlude that you two shared last night. But you don't have to fall in love because you got some good nookie. You don't have to love him to have sex with him, and you don't have to love him to enjoy having sex with him. The only thing you have to do is enjoy it (and please use a condom).

That's it. Cause it's not love. It's sex. Good sex, maybe. Real good sex, hopefully. But sex nonetheless. You are not making love. If you could make love by having sex, then we'd just keep having sex with them until we made them love us. But wait—that's exactly what we try to do, don't we?

And it doesn't work, does it?

## Sex, Love, and Making Love

I know what you're thinking: *So what you're saying, Ms. T., is that it's OK to go have sex without being in love?* What I'm saying is this: As hard as it may be to believe, I still basically advocate waiting to have sex until marriage, or at least until marriage is something the two of you have agreed on. It is the best way to guarantee that the person you have sex with is willing to commit to you.

That said, I just don't think it is realistic to expect that everyone will wait for the "real thing"—mutual love and marriage—before ever having sex. I think—and I'll admit I may be wrong on this point—sex is a way to express what you are feeling. When two people really love each other, having sex is a beautiful way to express that love. However, sex is also a way of expressing so many other feelings. Loneliness, anxiety, sadness, happiness, and yes, horniness can all be expressed through sex. And what is being expressed may or may not change each time you have sex. Every time two people who are in love have sex, they are not necessarily expressing their love. They may just want some, or they may be expressing one of the other feelings we mentioned.

So, do they ever "make love?" I don't know. I think they just express it. If you like to use the term "lovemaking" to express it, then use it. Just don't take it literally. The problem comes when we think that any act will "make love." *Love is not made*—at least not by any thing we do. Love is, or it is not. I'll go deeper into this when we talk about the player in love.

So have sex with him! Have fun and share your sense of humor with him. Have dinner and give him a taste of your cooking skills, or buy him dinner or let him buy you dinner. Share what you like with him. Share with him what he shares with you. Keep it fair. Fair exchange is no robbery. If he shares some sweet talk with you, share some back. If he shares his apple, share your orange. But keep your emotions to yourself. Why? *Because you don't know that he's sharing his emotions, too.* Until you can prove, beyond a shadow of a doubt, that he is *truly* sharing his emotions, then don't share yours.

## When and Why to Fake It
Faking emotions is just like faking orgasms. You fake it when you don't want him to know what you're

really feeling. You fake it when you don't know how to "not" respond. You fake it to shut him up. There are advantages to both showing fake emotions and showing no emotion at all.

Remember that the player always strives to get the most while giving the least. One thing that distinguishes the true player from the wannabe is that the player knows when he can back up without losing you. It's not a sixth sense; he knows because *you tell him*, by displaying the feelings you obviously have for him. The player uses your display of emotions as a gauge to determine where the game is in play. In the beginning, when there's no show of affection from you (either because you feel no affection yet or because you're still consciously trying to play it cool), the player is in pursuit mode. This means fun for you. But since the player does this often, he knows what to do in order to trigger an emotional response. When he doesn't get one, he adjusts the level of his game accordingly. More fun for you. If this continues, he will recognize that you're not responding to him like all the others did, and that's a problem for him. So if he's still interested, he revs his game up still further, maybe even to his "A" game level. This is the best of times for you. Enjoy the benefits that come with this pursuit.

Now: *this* is the point when you have to realize that once you start responding to his game by showing your emotions, he will know you're hooked. He will then proceed with the next phase, which is to back up. So the key at this point is to keep him chasing as long as he'll chase. If he gives up and walks away, he's either not feeling you enough to continue the pursuit, or he expects you to move closer to him once he moves away. Either way you should just chalk it up to over. You are not losing anything real because to this point he hasn't offered anything real. Even if it feels good, remember—it's just good game. But don't let that stop you from enjoying the chase as long as you can. It won't last forever, and it'll feel altogether different if you find yourself chasing him. Believe it.

There are benefits to faking emotions, but let me caution you first: don't try it if you think that you might have real feelings for this mug but you're trying to be cool about it. It is just too hard to display fake emotions when you are actually feeling him. Better that you get control of yourself and hold on tight to your emotions, or you'll get played. But if you're sure you're not feeling him, then showing some fake emotions can get some interesting results.

Since the player uses your display of emotion as the indicator that you are hooked, you will thus be able to observe how he proceeds to reel you in. Not by showing you more goodness (no—that's what we women do). Not by leaning closer to you and shortening the distance between you and him. No. He leans back to tighten up the line. This obvious retreat just when he knows he has you is one of the tell-tale ways to recognize that this is game and not just an indecisive brother. But I urge you, at this point, be careful. If he moves away, don't move toward him because you think you're in control. You've already found out what you needed to know. Stand your ground or move back. If he wants to continue to play, he'll move closer to you or at least stop backing up. If he doesn't, then let him go. You've gotten all the good that can come out of it. Only thing left is the bad.

It never ceases to amaze me how brothers complain constantly about women being too emotional. Think about the player who constantly asks the mark if she can handle this type of loose, uncommitted relationship. Yet he always wants to know if she's thinking about him or if there is anyone else in her life whom she might be feeling. For the player's game to work, the mark had better be emotionally invested. Just think: if we are able to remain emotionally detached, then players might actually have to do something to warrant our time and attention, as opposed to just receiving it because we care for them.

Remember this: you are uniquely wonderful, and your time and attention are valuable. Don't give it away for nothing. Make them earn it. Stay in control of your emotions. If you have to do a mantra every night, "I gots no love for you today, I gots no love for you today," then do it. Better yet, write it down fifty times every night. While you're driving, repeat it. "I gots no love for you today." When you're taking a break at work and he crosses your mind, remind yourself, "I gots no love for you today." When he calls you and says he was just thinking about you and wanted to hear your voice before he fell asleep, thank him sweetly, say goodnight, hang up the phone, and tell yourself, "I gots no love for you today." When you're out shopping for a gift for him for some holiday, say it before you get to the checkout line, "I gots no love for you today." (This will also save you some money.) When he gets finished knocking your boots off, and

I'm sure he will (players do seem to know how to knock some boots off), roll over and say thank you—but to yourself say, "I gots no love for you today. No love for you today, man. Instead, I'm gonna love me and protect me from you by not loving you. And I'm gonna do this until such time as I don't need protection from you. I WILL NOT LOVE YOU! OH NO! NOT TODAY!"

## Dealing with the Player's Words

In order to deal with a player without getting played, you will have to jam his game. Remember, each player has his own unique game. Even if he learned his game from another player, in order for it to work for him, he has to tailor it to his own specific skills, talents, and needs. But once developed, his game is his game. He may, at some point, have to upgrade his game to a higher level, but that's just an upgrade, not a redesign. Once comfortable that he has attained the mark, the player will revert to his holding game, the comfort zone where he feels most in control and gives least to the mark. Your goal is to keep him out of his comfort zone. (Which you should be able to do because you're emotionally in control and, well, because you're smarter.)

I cannot stress enough the importance of discerning when the player's words require a response and when they don't. The player knows that you'll say something back if he says something to you, so he says something—anything—to see how you'll respond.

The first thing to take into consideration is that unless he asks you a question, there really is no need to respond. Consider the following:

- "I would like to see you more often"—no response is really necessary.
- "Can I see you more often?"—a noncommittal "sure" or "we'll see" (or "hell no," as the case may be) is fine.
- "When and how can I see you more often?"— ah, now that's a real question.

And it deserves a question right back: "What do you mean, more often?" You need to know *exactly* what he's saying, and you need him to spell it out. Are we talking more occurrences of what you're presently doing (which might be fine depending on what you're presently doing)? Or are we looking at more by escalation of content? For example, what was a movie and dinner may escalate to dinner, a movie, drinks, and a walk in the park. What was a quick sexual encounter may escalate to an all-night love fest. (Be careful, though: you might not want him there in the A.M. looking for some bacon and eggs.)

When the player is throwing his word game at you, try to break it down to the concrete essence of what it really means. Is it a question or a statement? If it's a statement, is it a meaningful comment that you in turn should comment on, or a vague remark that requires little or no comeback? When in doubt, don't respond. Smile, laugh, say "oh" or "um," but don't agree or disagree, and for sure don't expound on it.

Why is it we feel we need to respond to any line the player lays on us? And when we do respond to some line that we're probably sure is untrue, why do we feel we have to be honorable and truthful with our response? I think it's because we want to be right, no matter what, so at the end, we can say, "I was straight up and honorable." Really? So what you are basically doing is honoring a lie. You are honoring game. Please, stop rewarding his bull with "honor." Instead, try giving him some bull in return.

Let's take a look at some typical player statements and some suggested responses.

*Statement: "Baby, you make me feel so good."*
*Response: "Oh yeah?" or "Me too! (that'll confuse him!)*

*Statement: "I think I might be ready to start thinking about settling down."*
*Response: "Oh yeah?"*

*Statement: "Baby, I want to take care of you."*
*Response: "Oh yeah?"*

Do you see where I'm going with this? Now let's look at some typical player questions of the bull variety—the kind that don't deserve any kind of real answers:

*Statement: "Sweetheart, were you thinking about me?*
*Response: "Why, were you thinking about me?"*

*Statement: "Are you seeing anyone else?"*
*Response: "Why, are you seeing anyone else?" or (my favorite) "Do you want me to see someone else? You need some help?"*

*Statement:* "Baby, do you need me to do anything for you?"

*Response:* "Yes, I need a couple hundred dollars for my trip with the girls to Jamaica. If you don't have the cash on you right now, I'll take your credit card or a check, but postdate it to the day you get paid. And oh, by the way, thank you."

The point is, unless the statement or question requires a legitimate response on your part, then respond to the words with *words* (and as few as possible), not *actions*. I was once told that most men only really listen to the first ten seconds of what a woman says. After that, they drift off into their own thoughts. So respond to him with six seconds or less of whatever, and let him listen to some dead air. That way, when you do have something to say, he won't be accustomed to tuning you out. He might actually listen because he's not used to you responding with much. The whole idea is to keep your reaction unfamiliar. Different from what he's accustomed to receiving. That way, you'll throw off his game.

### Dealing with the Player's Deeds

A little more finesse is necessary when responding to the player's deeds. He'll always give most generously of what he has most abundantly to give.

Whatever the deeds are, take care that you keep the following in mind:

1. The deeds are bait to get you hooked.
2. The deeds are bait to get you hooked! (Yep,

I know I repeated myself, but it's so important, I had to say it twice.)

3. When you are hooked, the deeds will significantly decrease, if not disappear altogether.
4. Your objective is to get the deeds without giving the player anything that he's not giving you.

The best way to slay the player's game is to stay in the zone where you're benefiting from the game without giving up your feelings or otherwise making yourself vulnerable. The key is to keep those deeds coming. But how? Well, if you understand that the deeds stop when you let the player know you're hooked, then—obviously—don't let him know. Whatever your response is to his deeds, make sure it is directly proportional to the effort required to do the deed. Here are some strategies for dealing with the deeds.

First, let's separate the deeds into four categories:

1. Things he gives you—gifts, money, jewelry, et cetera.
2. Things he does for you—cooking, home repairs, tax preparation, et cetera.
3. Thing he does with you—movies, dinners, vacations, amusement parks, et cetera.
4. Sex/physical contact—foreplay, oral, traditional, et cetera. This includes things like massages and hair washing. (Yes, in the beginning the veteran player will offer to wash your hair because he knows that to us, it feels better than a lot of the sex we've had in our lives. Also it's a great way to get at least your top off.)

### 1. Things He Gives You

The player shows up with a cute little ring on Valentine's Day or a basket of candy eggs on Easter. How do you respond? Well, let's see. Since the player generally doesn't stray too far away from his game, then the giving of the ring or Easter basket must be something he does often. He may have bought a box of cute little rings or several Easter baskets to give out for effect. Or he may obtain these gifts one at a time. But believe me, if he does it, it's not something that's hard for him to decide to do or that takes much effort. So when you receive these cute little trinkets, thank him. But thank him as if you're putting it in your collections of trinkets, and not as if you think it's a wedding band. Try, "Oh, this is nice—thanks." Not, "Oh my goodness, this was so unexpected! You are so nice and so thoughtful!"

Now, should those little rings turn into nicer jewelry, or that Easter basket turns into a flat-screen plasma television, you'll need to adjust your response accordingly. But remember, it's not about the value of the gift to you, it's about the value of the gift to him. Don't allow him to think you've fallen for him simply because of the gift he gives. But don't neglect to respond. His deeds always deserve a response, no matter how minimal. The player requires an acknowledgement from you that his efforts are appreciated and desired, even if he knows (and he knows) it didn't require much on his part. He may get perturbed if you don't respond as he expects you will, but trust that it's not because he thought that the gift was a big deal. It's because he thinks *his game* is a big deal, and you're not responding in a manner consistent with how others have responded. This throws his game off a bit. ~~Which is just what you want to do.~~

*Question: Wouldn't it be better to not respond at all, no matter what he gives? Wouldn't this completely throw his game off?*

Maybe, but this approach is very risky. The player may not wish to waste his time and talents and trinkets on a cold fish. The objective is to have him assume his game is working, but just not to the extent that it normally would at this stage. This brings out more effort. And don't forget: the player, as a player, has to play the game that he's mastered, and part of his game is to make you feel good. It's who he is. So when he increases his effort, he increases what he does for you that feels good, and consequently he increases the likelihood that you're gonna fall for him.

What can you do? Determine the level of the game and respond accordingly. If he assembled that Easter basket with his own hands, and it looks like he's not a pro at Easter basket assembly, then that player may have upgraded his game for you. He may even be pulling out his "A" game. Again, respond accordingly. Just don't let him think that you've fallen for him.

*Question: I'm a bit confused. How do I respond to the Easter basket?*

If it took a minimal amount of effort, then, "Thank you, that was a nice thing to do. Haven't had an Easter basket in years." If it appears that a significant amount of effort was involved (indicating that it's something he doesn't do often), then the response can be something like "Wow! What a nice thing to do. How very thoughtful of you. Maybe I'll bake you a dessert or something." Suggesting that you'll give him something in return for something he's given you is a good way for the player to know you appreciate the effort. Make sure it's something you can deliver with ease. Don't offer to cook if you can't or don't like to cook. Do what he does. Stay within your comfort zone, where you too are in control.

## 2. Things He Does for You

Let the player do whatever it is that he'll do for you. If you mention something you'd like done and he does it, then so be it. Recognize that when the player actually does something for you that does not directly benefit him, he will record it in his book of deeds. This is not so he can throw it in your face, but so he can have some inner justifications for his actions. Remember, the player thinks everything he does is a gift from the gods.

Your response to these deeds, again, should be in accordance to how much effort they took on his part. If the player is going to do something for you and it doesn't require you do something back, let him. Just thank him for doing it. This doesn't mean you have to do any more, or even as much, for him as he did for you. While the tables are turned in your favor, keep them there. Just say thank you.

If you're worried that a mere thank you will prevent him from doing any other deeds, then stop worrying. It's not gonna stop him, or keep him coming if he wants to stop. So spend less time worrying about how he's gonna feel about your reaction and more time concentrating on how you're gonna react. Control what you can control. You really can't control what he's gonna do for you or how he's gonna feel, so don't worry about it. Ask, if you want something done, but don't get upset if he doesn't do it. Keep in mind that whatever he's done for you was in your favor. You don't lose if he doesn't do for you. Unless, of course, your objective is to pile up the benefits. If that's the case, maybe you should pass this book to him.

### 3. Things He Does with You

The player's time is valuable, and he knows this because women are always jockeying for his time. There are maybe 99 women who would willingly give up 4 or more hours on a Friday night to go to a basketball game with him, whether they like basketball or not. But it doesn't follow that your making it 100 means your time should be valued at a 100 to 1 ratio to his time. No. Your hour is exactly equal to his hour—no more, no less. So the first thing to keep in mind as you look at the things he does with you is that he's not spending any more time with you than you're spending with him. The problems usually begin when he's spending all the time he *wants* to spend with you, but you're only spending all the time he'll *let* you spend with him.

Your objective is to ensure that *you* control the amount of time spent. If he wants to spend five hours with you, give him three. If he wants a weekend at the shore, give him an overnight. If he wants to talk on the phone with you, make sure you're the one who's "gotta go" first. Even if you're enjoying the conversation, cut it short on the brother. Make him feel like his glass isn't full yet. Keep him thirsty. Now that might honestly mean that you come out thirsty yourself. That's OK. Just don't let him know it. The player ain't having that; he will most likely turn the faucets on, so your cup will be running over with him. When he does, take most, but not all, of what you want. Don't drink him dry.

Make the player think about what to do with you. Let him expend some energy. A lot of the times, without our even recognizing it, we ask the player to do this or that with us. It'll come up in a conversation: "You never had corn fritters? Well, I know this restaurant that makes the best corn fritters, so we should go," or "The sequel to that movie that we liked comes out on Friday. We should go." In trying to move forward what you think is a promising relationship, you play right into the player's hands. You don't require that he even think about what makes you feel good—you just tell him what you want. Ladies, please stop this.

Trust, the player has a repertoire of what he will do with you. Let him put it on the table. Pick what you'd like to do with him and do it. Then you can work in what you want to do. Under no circumstances should you go back to those things you've eliminated because he's being so nice. He's just baiting you. He ain't nice. So don't do what you don't want to do with him.

This keeps you in the driver's seat. If he decides to move along because this isn't progressing to his liking, then let him move along. You have no regrets because you didn't go into this for him to stay. You did little or nothing of what you didn't want to do. And you gots no love for him today.

### 4. Sex

This is where what matters is how well you know yourself, not the player.

Before we get into this section, I'm gonna have to ask you to put your puritan cloak in the closet. If I'm grown enough to write about it, and you're grown enough to buy it, then we're both grown enough to talk about it honestly and openly. Let's be real. The title should have let you know that this book was gonna get down to the nitty-gritty at some point. I won't get too graphic or too carried away—I'll keep it rated "R." But I'm warning you. This part is critical. So stay with me.

There are two issues to discuss. Issue number one: are you ready for it? We know he's leading up to it. If you think he's not, then you're wrong. Doesn't matter what his approach is, he's leading up to it. So determine if you're ready for it. If you're not, then don't have sex. At the beginning of every date, decide if you're gonna have sex with him on this date. It is very important to determine this each and every time you are about to be with him. Make a decision about it before you see him and stick to it. No matter how the evening progresses. Just because he kissed your neck and it felt good doesn't mean you should have sex if you know you don't want to. You can enjoy the kissing as long as you're clear with yourself and with him that this is not leading to sex.

Now, that said, keep in mind that however far you went with the player the last time, he's gonna try to start right there, right where he left off, or else get right back there in a hurry. The preliminaries that he went through before, he will just glance over the next time. An hour of kissing before he touched your breast the last time will probably be two minutes of pecking and right to the boobs the next. Make sure you keep it at the stage that you are comfortable with. Assuming we're not all experienced "sex dodgers," the way to do this is just stop him (and yourself). Don't allow the sexual appetizers—the rubbing, the nibbling, the kissing, and whatnot—to go further than that. Just stop. Stand up. Pull your clothes back up or back down and just stop. If this sounds hard to do, just think about later on in your relationship with the player, when you really *want* to have sex with him, when you do everything in your power to turn him on, and he turns you down flat. Given the chance, he will. So turn him down now and don't give it a second thought. He'll recover. And so will you.

Issue number two: Giving him sex. If you give him sex, he *got* sex. You *gave* sex. Well—what did you get? What did you intend on getting? Satisfied? Not if your objective was to *give* him something. And I'll bet he got something. He got what you gave *and* he got what he came to get. Now, maybe you did get some physical satisfaction. But that will wear off as soon as you start to have second thoughts about the fact that you gave him some. And you will. Later on, you'll start to think, "Damn, maybe I shouldn't have given him any. Maybe I should have held back a little. Maybe he won't call me now that he's got sex. Maybe he's won."

You're damn right he's won. He won just as soon as you said you were gonna give him some. We throw that phrase around a lot. "Give him some." "Don't give him some." Why can't it be about getting some, not giving some? Let me get a bit raw here, ladies. Isn't the object of your having sex to get satisfied? To get off? If you get off, did he take anything from you? Did he get over on you?

For way too many years, it was just not important whether women enjoyed sex. It was our obligation, and if we happened to enjoy it, we were just lucky and we kept it to ourselves. In fact, those of us who did enjoy sex were frowned upon. They were considered "loose." Well, we've loosened up quite a bit since those times. We ain't got no business having sex we don't enjoy.

Now, I know sometimes we get a bad batch. Sometimes we're in such a foul mood that Denzel himself couldn't make us feel good. (Man, I hope I'm never feeling that foul, you hear me!) But the objective should be to enjoy it. There ain't no robbery when it's a fair exchange. Nobody gave anybody anything they didn't get. If you can think about sex like that, then you won't have those regrets later. You won't have to second-guess whether you gave in too soon. If you go into it to get satisfied, and you get satisfied, then it's all good. You didn't give in to him. You got some sex. If you're honest with yourself, you might admit that you needed some sex.

One good thing about most players, especially at the early stages of the game, is that not only are they absolutely good at sex, they want to make it good for you, too. They are so confident about their sexual prowess that they will do whatever's necessary to ensure that you walk away feeling "wow!" What better time to enjoy it? I say, go ahead and get some.

Never forget, though—good sex is *just* good sex. It is not making love, making like, or making anything else except making you physically satisfied. Don't get emotional about it, even if he's done things to you that no one's ever done. Even if he hit the spot that time forgot. He is a player! Of course he knows how to hit it. It's what he does time and time and time again. So don't be fooled. Just enjoy it and walk away with a smile on your face saying—what? "I gots no love for you today."

Once you control the power that comes with taking charge of your sexuality, the player can't use it against you. He can no longer persuade you to have sex simply because he's done nice things for you. Sex is not a reward. When he's disappeared for a while and shows up only to have sex, you decide if you want to get some from him or not. If you don't, say "See ya!" If you do, go ahead and get some. Then say "See ya!" That's all he's offered, so that's all you can get. He won't be trying to rekindle the romance that you had when he was baiting you. He's just trying to hit it to keep you on standby. Recognize this. Decide if sexual standby is OK with you. If not, move on.

### Dealing with Persistent Game

OK—let's say you're following the slayer route I've laid out for you here. You're playing well. You're in control. You see him when you want to see him. If and when you had sex, it was your decision. You have not allowed him to pressure you into playing the game his way. Sometimes the player walks away at this point. Sometimes the player doesn't walk away. Sometimes even if he's feeling that his game isn't working quite the way he'd like it to, he isn't ready to throw in the towel. It may be pride. It may be that he's invested a lot into this game and wants to be rewarded for his efforts. Or it just may be that he wants to attain this particular mark. Whatever the reason, he's hanging in there. Understand that hanging in there doesn't require any surge of effort—he's just increasing the level of the game as need be.

He keeps marching forward. He doesn't get dissuaded or disillusioned. If he does, he doesn't show it. He keeps on doing the right things and saying the right things. He wants you and he wants you to know it. Months go by and he's still pursuing you. But you're slayer enough to know that this could be game, so you stand your ground and refuse to fall for his charms. Every now and then the player erupts into an Oscar-worthy performance portraying the innocent victim: "What do I have to do? I'm trying so very hard, but you keep shooting me down. You know I like you. If I didn't, I'd have been gone long ago!"

But keep in mind that no matter how dogmatic he appears to be about obtaining you, you are probably not the only mark on his dance card. He has the luxury of waiting on you because someone (or -ones) else is tending to his needs. The fact that you are not responding as he would like isn't shaking the foundation of his universe. It's just shaking up that compartment of his life where he houses the game he's trying to play on you. When you see his agitated response caused by the fact that he "just can't win with you!" understand that it means just that. He's frustrated because he's not winning. Don't confuse it with frustration due to his being unable to prove to you that he really cares for you. That would mean it might not be game.

Trust, if it's not game you'll eventually find out. But game doesn't have an expiration date on it. The answer to "If I wasn't really interested, would I still be here?" is yes. It's like layaway. He assumes he'll get his rewards in the end, even if it takes a little longer than usual to pay on it.

The persistent game usually ends in the player attaining the mark because the mark is likely to believe that longevity equals sincerity. It doesn't. The brother is just long-winded. That's all. So if he's waiting, keep him waiting. Stay in this phase of the game until you want more or less, or until he gives up.

## A Note on the Married Player

I am perpetually astounded by the number of players who are married. They wait for the question. The question might not come for days. Women ask all around the question: "What are you doing for Christmas?" "When is the last time you went to the movies?" "I hate waking up in the middle of the night to a cold lonely bed, don't you?" The *real* question is, "Are you married?" The player who lives with his woman will quickly answer no to the question of marriage, but will stutter over the subject of whether he lives with someone.

I'm finding more and more that if you just ask, you'll get an honest answer. Don't get me wrong—they're not running up to women shouting "Hi! I'm married! Wanna date?" But they're not putting their rings in their pockets, either.

Of course, many players are still keeping their home relationships, if they have them, a secret. Regardless, don't be surprised when you find out that some of the mackingest brothers in the club are married and no one knows. These players may have been around for years, but the issue of their marriage or live-in girlfriends never really gets cleared. When asked, these players might just answer with the overused, "What's that got to do with us?" Similarly, the player who wears his wedding ring may also respond with, "What's that got to do with us?" To go one better, some players announce very early on and without provocation, "Yeah, I'm married. But what's that got to do with us?"

But what blows me away, what absolutely floors me, are the sistas who don't know—or don't care— what it has to do with them.

I attended the Million Woman March a few years back, and I can remember thinking that if this group here, just these women, could collectively decide to leave other women's husbands alone, then we would have served a devastating blow to the game. Just imagine, if you would. All the married men (including the men who are not married, but go home to the same woman every night) sitting on one side of the club. No flirting going on over on that side of the room. Why, they might actually have to be satisfied with drinking, dancing, and going home. The plus side for these married brothers would be that because their wives are aware of the pact the sistas have made, and thus don't have to worry about their husbands playing, they would be much more agreeable to allowing their men go out. (Or at least they should be. Sistas, we got some stuff with us, too. But that's another book). Even the single players should support this notion, as it increases the available pool of marks.

I don't really expect the "stay away from their men" pact to take place. But. Ladies. If he says he's married and he and his wife are together, leave him alone. If he says he's not married but is in a live-in relationship, leave him alone. If you've been seeing him for a while and you find out he's married, leave him alone. If he's good to you and fine and sweet and wonderful, but he has someone else at home, leave him alone. I know there are not a lot of qualified men out there, but ladies, the married ones are definitely NOT qualified. Even if you just want to hit it with him, just think of how you'd feel if someone wanted to hit it with your man. Respect your fellow sistas. As soon as you find out he's got someone at home—no matter what story he comes up with, no matter how hard he says things are at home, no matter how much she doesn't understand him or is cheating on him or doesn't want him anymore—leave him alone.

## Dealing with Indisputable, Undeniable, In-Your-Face Game

That guy is a capital-P Player! Look at him in that girl's face over there. He was just in that other girl's face. It looks like they're all just waiting their turn! He's just taking numbers. He ain't even buying no drinks. He ain't even that cute! Who does he thinks he is?

A Player. My own personal favorite kind. He knows

who he is and he LOVES it. No deception. No cloak and dagger. He doesn't need you to think that he wants a relationship. He doesn't have to wine you and dine you and convince you that he's an OK brother. He does not have to disguise the fact that you are about to be played. Remember the fighters who would tell their opponents that they were about to get hit with an overhand right, and then hit them with an overhand right? This type of player does not feel you have any defense against his game.

The best thing to do if you decide to play with him is to decide what you want out of it. *Please* don't think you're gonna change him. Just understand that for the player to be this confident, he must be that good. If you feel you want to enjoy his goodness, then do so. But let him know up front. Tell him that this is just for kicks. Just a taste test, as it were. And do just that. Taste it and go. Don't mess around with this player too long. You'll end up with a dunce cap on, wondering how you let him get to you when you knew better.

## When the Game Feels Good

No matter what type of player you're dealing with, you'll find yourself at a point when playing with him just feels good. I've said this before, and I'll say it again: *of course* it feels good. Ensuring that it feels good is what the player does.

There is nothing wrong with experiencing the goodness. In fact, that is the only legitimate reason to play with the player. Just keep your wits about you (and this book in your bag beside you). Keep your girls close. This is not the time to shy away from your friends while you bask in the joy and light of his sun-shine. This is when you need your girls. Make sure you have at least one level-headed friend who you can talk to honestly. Make sure she too has a copy of this book.

This is also not the time to put your hobbies and interests to the side. All too often we cancel ladies' night out, or stop going to the gym, or slow up on our projects because we just want to sit by and make ourselves available to him. (Careful. "Sit by" is very close to "stand by," isn't it?) Continue having a life where your happiness and enjoyment is not predicated on him and his moves. I hope by now you've learned that the good doesn't last long with the player. Remember the woman who left her own garden to attend to his. Continue being you. Continue enjoying you. Make the player a small part of your life. That way, when he's gone, it won't matter so much.

## Dealing with the Player in Public

I know we shouldn't care what people think of us. But ladies, come on. The player is not your man. So don't parade him as if he is. Don't walk around on his arm like you're the Queen of Sheba, giving all the women the look that says, "I know you want him. You may have already had him. But he's mine now." He's not yours. He might acquire you, but you're not going to acquire him. So don't front. Because in a couple of months, when your great run is reduced to a slow crawl, you'll wish you'd never been seen with him. And actually, playing it cool and not letting the outside world know you're seeing the player might extend the "fun" period. So keep it quiet. Tell him,

"Yo player, we don't have any reason to advertise, do we?" (I just love calling them players to their face—they hate that!) The player has got to appear that he's winning. Broadcasting your capture will only increase his stock. And you'll walk away with your head down wondering how you got played again.

## A One-Player Woman—A Little More Q&A

*Question: Should I be in a monogamous relationship with the player?*

No. Don't be monogamous. There is no legitimate reason to be monogamous with someone else who is not.

*Question: Should I be dealing with two or more players at a time?*

Two players at a time is just a juggling game. It's like playing bingo with more than one card. It takes the pressure off. Now, consider: does this make you a player? Hmmm. This is a very fine line. I think that if you're comfortable with this, then do it. There are no innocents here. No one is looking for a relationship. And you're protecting yourself. It is much easier to control your emotions when you're not focused on one person.

*Question: Can I play with the player and a nice guy at the same time?*

If you have established that one of the men that you are dealing with is a nice guy who wants a relationship, and you want to pursue the possibility of a relationship with him, then leave the player alone. Don't keep him as a backup. But if you don't want a relationship with the nice guy, then leave him alone. Let him find someone to appreciate him. Else this book is about you.

If you're dealing with two or more guys, whether they are two players or two nice guys, I hope this means that you are not really serious about either of them. If one or both men are nice guys, make sure that neither of them thinks that they are in a monogamous relationship. That's not cool, and you don't want someone to have to slay *your* game. If one or all are players, it doesn't really matter what they think.

If you're looking for a nice guy and you think you've found one, give him time and don't rush it. If he's really a nice guy, his true colors will shine through whether you have your guard up or not. So keep it up.

## When the Game Is Not So Good

Even while it's good there will be times when it's not so good. There will be times when his mind is on something or someone else. He may say or do things that don't feel good to you. You can minimize these times by remembering one simple fact: You are not a toilet. If he needs to dump on someone, he'd better find another holding tank. Do not let him get into a pattern of saying or doing anything he wants to do to you. (A pattern in this case means "more than once.") If you let him get away with it more than once without speaking on it, then you'll become his dumping ground. Let him take that somewhere else.

This might not be sounding like much fun now. I know that most books would tell you to leave the player alone entirely. Well, as I've said before, this ain't that kinda book.

## When You Should Not Play

I have counseled you on how and when to play. But I need to spend a moment on when *not* to play.

1. Never play when you are at the end of a bad relationship. Your wounds are fresh and wide open. And believe me, a player will pour salt into them, just because he can. Take some time and pull yourself together. Find a way to be OK about your new situation. Get past lonely. Remember that the worst thing that can happen to you in the world of love is not that you end up alone, it's that you end up alone and you aren't OK with it. Definitely make sure you're OK before you deal with a player. If not, well, let's just say it could get awfully ugly.

2. Never play with a player if it's been a long time since you dealt with anyone at all. Find something or someone to take the edge off before you go trying your new skills and confidence out on a player. (You know how they tell you not to go shopping on an empty stomach?) I had a player once tell me never to go out into the world with a loaded gun—I might shoot it at the first target I run across. (Of course he followed that bit of advice up by unselfishly offering himself to use for target practice.) Whatever it is that you need to do, do it. If you are unable to find someone

or something to relieve the pressure that you are under, then stay in the house until you do. Don't walk into the player's arena tight and tense.

3. Do not enter into the game with the *objective* of playing the players. Even bona fide players aren't looking to play the players. They may not run away from the challenge of another player, but that's not what they run out of their doors looking for. They venture out to play marks. Therefore your objective should not be to play the player; *your objective is to not get played.* Just as the player's objective is to win, your objective is to not lose. If the objective is to not lose, and you don't lose, then you've achieved your objective; in essence, you win. But if your objective is to conquer the player and make him your mark, you will probably lose—unless you've turned into a player yourself. But be careful: the nice ones might be armed with a copy of this book in their back pockets.

# Five ‖ When to Get Out of the Game

BY NOW YOU'VE GOTTEN a lot of information about the game and how it's played, and thus you're a lot less vulnerable to the nonsense. You're more aware of the mechanics of the game, the cause and effect of the moves made; you've gotten your strategy together and you're ready to play a few hands with the player. You're almost ready: there's just one more lesson to learn.

When you walk into a casino, you know that it is not in the business of losing money. Even if you walk out with a wheelbarrow full of loot, you know that the casino did not lose money that night. It just didn't win against you. And if you had stayed and played longer, the odds are that you would not have come out a winner at all. The house will always win if you play too long.

The longer you play with the player, the more you increase his chances of playing you. He will eventually find your weaknesses and use them against you. His persistence will defeat your resistance, and he will break you down. The longer you stay, the more likely you'll become attached to him emotionally.

Once that happens, that tight game you were playing will begin to crack. You'll begin to respond to his deeds with deeds, and then respond to his words with deeds. You'll begin to forgive the occasional (though more frequent) changes in his behavior—lack of consideration, increasing forgetfulness, waning desire to see you. Just momentary lapses, you'll think. You'll move a little closer to him to close the gap as he moves a little further away. Next thing you know—WHAM! You're played.

It may be enticing to hang in there when things are going your way. It may actually appear that he is really feeling you. And maybe he is. (I promise, I *will* talk about the player in love.) But that doesn't mean he won't play you the first chance he gets. He will. Your best defense against getting played, once you're in the game, is to know when it's time to leave.

*Question: Ms. T., how do I know when it's time to get out?*

In any relationship, in order to understand what is changing and how it is changing, you need to have a clear knowledge of where things were before you suspected that they had changed. So get out your calendars, ladies. After your first real date with a player, begin to keep a record of what he does and when he does it. *All of it.* Every actual deed—the gifts, the time spent, the telephone calls he initiates (though not the conversation itself—that's just words), the dinners, the things he fixes for you, everything. It doesn't have to be detailed, just a notation: PC = phone call, EV = evening date, DD = daytime date, GT = any type of gift, FX = fixing something, SX = Sex, GSX = good sex, GTSX = great sex. (Definitely track the sex! If nothing else, you may be surprised at how often or how little you're actually getting some.) You'll be able to see at a glance when things begin to trail off, which will make it harder for you to justify or excuse what he is doing or not doing.

It might even be helpful to set some goals for yourself as to when you'll bow out, such as if he doesn't call after seven days, or if he hasn't asked you out in three weeks. If the only interaction you've had with him in more than a month has been his popping over for sex, and this is different than the kinds of activity you've shared over the previous couple of months, then it may be time to go. And *really* go, ladies.

Need still more help? Here are my ten foolproof signs that will let you know when it's time to go:

1. When he stops trying to spoon you all night. (You know what spooning is, don't you— lying together with your bodies in line with eachother, like spoons.)
2. When he insists that the only night he's available is the night he knows that you've always designated as Girls' Night Out.
3. When he only calls as a response to your call.
4. When the last three suggestions of what the two of you could do for fun came from you.
5. When he was not interested in your last three suggestions of what the two of you could do and he had none of his own.
6. When he stopped answering your midnight booty call.
7. When the last thing he really did for you was to make your life easier by telling you specifically what he wanted for his birthday.
8. When he makes no specific plans to see you on his birthday, but shows up the next day for his gift.

9. When his half-ass confirmations continually result in no-shows.
10. When it just ain't fun anymore.

If it ain't fun, and it ain't prosperous, then why stay? Because it has potential? Because it was fun before? Stop kidding yourself. Just go. Get on out of there.

And don't talk about it. Just *be* about it. I have been told by more than a few brothers that women talk entirely too much. It is our downfall. When we get in a relationship, we give them all the details about our last relationships and how they went wrong. When we're in the middle of the relationship, we tell them every move we've made or are about to make. When we end a relationship, we make sure we let them know exactly why we're leaving. What do we gain by giving all this info? Nothing. They just use it all against us!

Now I ask you. Is that how you win at games? You've played games before, right? Monopoly, chess, poker, football, hide-and-go-seek—in what game did you give your opponent (and the player definitely sees *you* as his opponent) this much info on exactly what he needed to do to win? Which sport gives the opposing team their playbook? Also, when the game is over, either by win, lose, draw, or quit, isn't it obvious? Doesn't it stand to reason that if one of the participants is no longer participating in the game, then the game is over?

When you leave the player, you don't have to announce it. Just go. It isn't necessary that he recognize it immediately. It isn't necessary that he understands what he's lost. He doesn't need to know what he's done wrong. You're not leaving to teach him a lesson. You're not leaving to affect him. You're leaving to keep from getting played. The best way to slay the player and truly jam his game is to leave before he makes a loser out of you.

# Six ‖ The Player Gets Caught Up

IN A CONVERSATION I had with a player who had recently gotten married, he informed me that his relationship with his wife started out as game. When I asked what happened, he responded, "I got caught up." Getting caught up in the game is what happens to a player when he falls in love with the mark.

Before we look at the phenomenon of the caught-up player, let's take an honest look at love. As human beings, we want and need love. We want to see it in the movies, hear it in our music, and read it in our literature. There is a great deal written on the practice of love, how it feels to be truly loved, how one acts and behaves when truly in love. Real love feels wonderful. To go one step further: if it hurts, then by definition it is not love. If someone hurts you, or treats you badly, or makes you sad by their actions, then that person does not love you.

I will not get into how love is defined. If you need a definition of love, then put this book down for a minute and go explore the subject of love. What I will address here is how love is practiced. More specifically, what one does when one is in love.

My fundamental feeling on love is this:

Love is. Or it is not.

One more time:

**LOVE IS! OR IT IS NOT!**

Ideally, every time you love someone, you treat them with affection, consideration, attention, and respect. Ideally, every time someone loves you, they treat you the same way.

*Question: Well Ms. T., maybe he didn't love me because he didn't treat me right, but I loved him because I treated him right. Right?*

No. Not right. And who are you to say if that person loved you or not? All you can do is surmise. Only he knows for sure. You only know if you *felt* loved by him.

Love is. Or it is not. Have you ever been involved with someone who treated you good? Real good? Just like you wanted to be treated? But you didn't and couldn't love him, even though you knew it was in your best interest to do so?

Have you ever been involved with someone who treated you like dirt, and no matter how you tried to get him out of your mind and heart, you couldn't? Because you loved him and wished you didn't?

When was the last time you told your heart, "Heart, today we're gonna fall in love with *that* guy," and your heart listened? It doesn't work that way. You just love. One day you look up and you've fallen in love. Falling out of love is the same way.

Furthermore, your actions and behaviors are not dictated by love. We would like them to be, but they aren't. When you love, you love, whether you treat the one you love like royalty or like an unwanted dog. Who you are as a person is much more likely to govern how you react and behave in love, than the fact that you're in love.

But I think that love's greatest power lies in the fact that it intensifies the highs and the lows, the good and the bad, the happy and the sad that we experience while in love. That breakfast in bed that he fixed for you tasted better because you love him. That hug he gave you was warmer because you love him. That argument last night was more bitter because those words of anger were coming from and going to someone you love. New Year's Eve alone was infinitely lonelier because there was someone you love who you weren't with.

And sex! Good sex with the one you love is heaven on earth! Consequently bad sex—well, bad sex with the one you love is still kinda alright. But no sex from the one you love is awful!!!! Now if Johnny, who you are not in love with, doesn't want to give you some, so what? But if Billy, whose bath water you would gladly drink, turns down your offer of some hot butt-naked lovin', well that's just the end of the world.

OK, this is all *very* important, so let's recap:

- Being in love doesn't guarantee you'll behave in a loving manner.
- Behaving in a loving manner doesn't mean you're in love.
- When love is, love is, regardless of how you act or what you do.
- Love intensifies the feelings that result from the actions and experiences that transpire while one is in love.

*Question: Ms. T.—this is all very important, and thank you for it. But that player who married his mark—how did he fall in love? What did the mark do to make him fall in love? What is the secret to making the player fall in love? Was it something she did?*

*What was going on in the player's life to make him vulnerable to love? Ms. T., you've got to tell us what to do to make the player fall in love!*

The truth of the matter is that when the player falls in love, it's really no different than when anyone falls in love. There's no real answer as to why the player, after having countless women, falls in love and marries one. I guess it's the same reason why anyone falls in love. They just do.

(But I will tell you this. This particular mark I know of was proposed to before, by another serious player. He had marked and played her, but at some point he got caught up. She turned him down and left him, breaking his caught-up player heart. She later met the player [*big-time* player] who she eventually married. I guess she must have known some secrets.)

So when the player falls in love, and realizes that he's in love, he does just what any of us would do in that situation. He tries to lock it down. To own it. Nobody wants the person we love to get away from us. The player "queens" the mark and makes her his number one. He may decide to live with this queened mark; he may even marry her. But whatever he decides to do, he does it because he doesn't want her to get away.

If the queened mark leaves the player, what would have been just a momentary void that could be filled by another mark now becomes an unacceptable loss. Even though women leave him all the time, the player is not willing to let this queened mark leave. This is how he gets caught up. What he does for, to, and with this mark now moves well outside of his "A" game. He gets caught up by doing whatever is necessary to lock the mark down. And most of the time, he succeeds. Making a woman fall for him, especially when it really matters, isn't the hardest challenge for the player.

Before you know it, he's in a real relationship. Now, does he change his playin' ways, give up the game, and settle down?

How I wish I could tell you it is as simple as that. The player is not likely to change just like that. After all, he is who he is.

More than likely, in the beginning he will enjoy the company of his queen, primarily. After all, he loves her and he wants to enjoy her and the love he feels for her. There's no telling how long this honeymoon will last. What usually ends it, though, is the reappearance of real life and the issues that naturally arise when two people decide to share one space. The couple must then develop the pattern that will be their normal relationship.

Now, what is normal for the player? Normal for the player is the game. When his life starts to get uncomfortable—regardless of the source of that discomfort—the player will seek out the familiar and comfortable. He resorts to the thing that he knows he is good at. He slides back into the game.

Some players never completely leave it. Most always have a least one standby mark who will be there whenever he calls, even if he doesn't call for years. When and if he ever gets back to her, she'll drop whatever's going on in her life and make herself available. So the player finds it easy to resume his game, though it will require more than a bit of discretion.

The player's advantage is that he is accustomed to juggling women and coming up with creative excuses. He develops a pattern of giving the queen enough (sometimes barely enough) of what she needs so that she won't leave him. The queen may or may not be happy, but as long as she doesn't leave the relationship, the player is satisfied. He has his lifestyle and all its pleasures, and he has his love. If someday he grows weary of the game or is forced out of it for whatever reasons (i.e. sickness, age), he already has a relationship that he can count on. He invested in love when it came along, and now he has it in his stock portfolio. He'll utilize the dividends, feeling secure in the knowledge that he has the principal to cash in when the day comes that he just wants a one-on-one relationship.

*Question: It seems like getting caught up in the game works out well for a player, his way of having his cake and eating it too. Why then isn't falling in love at least one of the player's objectives?*
If falling in love were the player's objective, then he wouldn't be a player. The player is not looking for love. He's looking to satisfy his desire to conquer this particular woman at this particular time. When the player gets caught up and finds himself in love, it's only because, contrary to popular belief, the player is human. (Yes, I'm sure.)

*Question: Ms. T., why doesn't the player take this opportunity to get out of the game? Doesn't he worry that his playin' antics will cause him to lose the queen he loves?*
The player in love absolutely believes he can handle both love *and* the game. Not only is there no ur-

gency for him to get out of the game, there is no real reason for him to stop. This is actually the game at maximum velocity.

*Question: Ms. T., why does the mark allow herself to be queened by the player? Isn't it bad enough that she was marked? Doesn't she recognize him for who he is? Assuming she's a woman of at least marginal intelligence, why in heaven's name would she marry him?* Before we put this sister down, let's look at it from her perspective. Even if she knows her man is a player and she was his mark, what part of his game is marriage? Unless he's been married a bunch of times, marriage is outside of the realm of his game. And unless the mark has a lot of money, then it's a good bet that the player is marrying her because he loves her. The mark knows this. To her, he's caught. In all actuality, he's just caught up. What's the difference?

Let's say the player is a big fish. Many fisherwomen throw their hooks out with their best bait. (I know I switched the fish and bait thing around, but just stay with me.) The biggest and best player fish manage to eat all the bait on all the lines without ever getting hooked. Now along comes Fisherwoman "Q." Ms. Q. has a good combination of the right bait and the right-sized hook. She throws it in at the right time, maybe under the right light or water conditions. The player fish takes a nibble, likes it, and keeps on nibbling. He doesn't really realize or even care that he's dangerously close to biting down on the hook. He keeps nibbling until WHAM! He's hooked.

Now Ms. Q. starts to reel him in. And he lets her. It's not because he's hooked so securely that he can't break free—he's just enjoying the taste of that bait. And besides, he's confident he can shake free at any time. All the other fisherwomen see that the big fish is on her hook and is not really trying to get away.

Now this is a big fish, and even though he's on her line, he's too big and has too much energy to be just pulled into the boat. So she throws a net over him, and he holds still for it, as if he wants to be pulled into the boat. The net's big enough for him to move around in. Ms. Q. gives him plenty of extra line, because, after all, the net is over him. But unknown to her, the big fish has made a hole in the net—a hole big enough to be able to nibble on another fisherwoman's piece of bait comin' by if he so chooses. Even though she's continually giving him the bait of his choice, the player fish still nibbles on outside bait as it floats by the net.

And don't think for a minute the other fisherwomen stop trying to catch this fish. They actually try harder, because now they know the big fish is capable of being caught. They suspect it's just a matter of time before he wiggles off of Ms. Q.'s line and onto theirs. He's caught up, but still managing both his game and his love. However, Ms. Q. thinks he's caught. There is no reason for her not to pull up her other fishing poles and devote her efforts to this big fish.

When the player is *truly* caught, he will remove all of the other miscellaneous marks from his life. And the likelihood that the player will someday give up the game (if he lives long enough) is very high. So if this queened mark can hang in there, then she will probably catch the player. But the problem is when? How long can she be expected to hang in there? He may not be ready or willing to give up the game for years and years and *years*. How much can she endure before she has to leave? Whether it's because she has fallen out of love with him, or because even though she does still love him she has to leave to protect herself, one thing is for sure. The prolonged extracurricular activity of the player has a devastating effect on the queened mark. I've known many who found a way to stay, and many who had to go. It comes down to the fear factor: fear of leaving versus fear of staying.

Whatever the outcome, the reality is that the player does love the queened mark. But love didn't make him leave the game. Remember the player that I told you about who married his mark? Well, he didn't stop his playin' ways, and guess what? She left him. His love for her and her love for him had nothing to do with it (and trust me, they had some mad love for each other). Who he was, and what she could ultimately no longer tolerate, decided their fate.

*Question: Ms. T., how does the player in love behave?*
A tiger doesn't change his stripes just because he's caged. When the player is caught up and inside of a relationship, he did not get into that relationship to satisfy the wants and needs of his queen. He got in for himself, because *he* wanted to. His queen should not expect him to be considerate and responsible just because he committed. He won't be mowing the lawn, or cooking dinner, or helping with the grocery shopping, or painting the fence if he wasn't doing those things as part of his normal routine when he was single. As a matter of fact, he will probably do

much less, expecting her to take care of him like he's accustomed to being cared for, even though before he was being cared for by many. What he'll do when he's home is sleep or watch TV or whatever else he likes to do to occupy his time when he's home. He's not cuddling with his queen and watching movies, even if he used to come over and do it. That was game. This is life. He's there now. What else could she possibly want from him?

He's not going to be a homebody. He'll still have plenty of things to do and plenty of places he still has to go to do them. He will go—and he will go frequently. He will probably respect curfew—you know, don't let the sun beat you home. But just because he's caught up doesn't mean he'll be caught in.

And don't expect him to take his queen out regularly or accompany her to weddings or family picnics or outings of that nature. He will attend only those affairs he wants to go to and that's that. Oh, she may argue enough to get him to go her cousin's wedding, but chances are when they get there he's going to act so bored and uninterested that she will hesitate to force him to go with her again. That's what he does. The player is, and that doesn't change because he's caught-up.

OK, it seems as if the player doesn't really want to be bothered all that much with his queen. So you'd think he wouldn't mind if she had a life of her own. Hobbies, friends, interests. Things to occupy her time and keep her out of his hair. Nope. He doesn't want his queen out there having fun and possibly being influenced by others. The player expects his queen to be home and at his disposal. He will make it his business to throw a monkey wrench into whatever interests she may have. He wants her dependent on him for entertainment, even though he's not likely to supply enough of it himself. He will keep her wanting. That way she'll be satisfied with the morsels he gives her. Same game that he's always played.

Well, at least she's got him for sex, right? Ha! Sex may start out hard and heavy, but it will dwindle. The player does not necessarily equate sex with love. So though he loves her, he may not want to have sex with her, and he may only do it because he knows it's required, or because something turned him on (maybe her, maybe not) and she was there.

Does the caught-up player cheat? Yep. He may have a dry spell and sincerely try to do the right thing. But as I've said before, when life gets uncomfortable, he will revert to that which makes him comfortable. The game.

*Question: Ms. T. So what should I do if I find that the player I'm involved with is in love with me and maybe wants to marry me?*
Pray.

# Seven | In Closing

STILL THINK YOU WANT to climb in the ring and go toe to toe with the player? Well, nothing slays a player like a mark playing *his* game on *her* terms. I hope you now know how to prepare yourself in case that next nice guy turns out to be a player. Because chances are, you'll never know until you know.

Slaying the player isn't about getting what you can get. It's about forcing the game to be fair to you. It's about being honest and clear, about getting and giving the same, and no more, in return. If the player is giving you time, then give him time. If the player is giving you words, then give him words right back. Playing with the player does not mean you take, take, take. Because believe me, any player worth his salt will not let you take take, take, take unless he has a master plan already in play.

I have just a few points I'd like to reiterate. They're not in any particular order but are all worth reviewing:

- Remember to differentiate words from deeds. Words are just words. Don't get overly carried away by them.
- Don't react to words with deeds. React to them with words or nothing at all.
- Remember to evaluate the player's deeds based on their value to the player, not on their value to you. Do not surmise that because he did something nice, he is therefore nice. He ain't nice. He's a player.

- Remember not to confuse acting in a loving manner with love. The key word here being "acting." When love comes it will stand up to the test. Love will make itself known. But until you're sure it's love, treat it like it's game.

- Don't think that you'll make him change his playin' ways. Only he can change himself, and only in his time. Not yours.

- Remember to keep a chart documenting his deeds. It's the easiest way to know when they've stopped. Otherwise you may be too engulfed in the game to notice.

- Remember that if you don't allow him to dump on you, he will hold it in or dump it somewhere else. Don't let him unload it on you.

- Don't give anything you don't want to give, when you don't want to give it.

- Remember to keep your love for yourself. Don't give it to the player. Remember to say to yourself—out loud, so you can hear it— "I GOT'S NO LOVE FOR YOU TODAY!"

Most importantly, know when it's time to go. Know that there's no shame or blame in leaving someone who isn't good to you or for you. I heard someone say, "The strong give up and move along, while the weak give up and stay." Stay strong, my sistas.

Peace,
Ms. T.

# Acknowledgments

First and foremost I'd like to praise God for his mercy and blessings. I am nothing without His love. I am nothing without His love.

A very special thanks to Doug Seibold at Agate for pulling The Slayer out of the pile and believing in it.

There are many people who have been supportive of me during the course of the writing of this book. If I missed anyone, please charge it to my head and not to my heart.

I'll start with my "Posse," as it is my relationship with them that ignited the fire that brought forth *The Player Slayer*. Warm love and thanks to Tracela, Keith, Pace, Zac, Shawn, Chris, and Fredrick. Special thanks to Frank at "Cut It Out" for the colors! Shout-outs to the folks at O'Hara's: Les, Ann, Dwayne, Clay, DJ Rick, and all the regulars. To my coworkers: Ira, Dave, Joel, Dan, Regina, Cathy, Trisha, Deb, and Daniel, who deal with my nonsense on a day-to-day. Mad love to Suzanne and Andrea ("Budd") for their early and much appreciated edits and comments. To the voices: Chris and Artis—thanks players (I'm sorry—ex-players)!

Of course I must acknowledge the players. But rather than hate, I'll just give initials: SP, HB, PE, DC, GJ, LB, uncle JB, RG, QC, and all the others whose complete initials I can't provide but whose game needs to be recognized. Thanks for the data.

Kathleen and Karen, my friends for most of my life, and without whom there would surely be anarchy. And who wants that? (I do, I do.) To my "road dog," Laura. We sure learned how to "fake it till you make it!" Love and peace, my sister. To the brothers who rescued me with their friendship, kindness, advice, support, shoulders, food, and, well, whatever else, when I so desperately needed it: SaKeem— thanks, "boodah," Terry, Donald, Don, and Mike. To Manning, who owes me three fish sandwiches, thanks for all of the above. To Maurice "Mo" Cheeks whom I have loved (unrequitedly and anonymously) for way too long. Holla back.

To my family (and y'all know I'm not naming all y'all): Sheila, Charles "Man," Charles "Chuck," Marquan, Troi, Michelle, Chaunclyn, Zaynah, Butter, Storm, Trina, Big Jim, Suden, and the rest. To my mother- and father-in-law, Charlotte and Vernon, thank you for all the love and guidance you continue to show me, even after. Thanks for being my parents too. To "Gizmo" and "Stripe," my constant companions. I loved-d-d those dogs, baby!

To Paul, I guess that which doesn't kill you makes you stronger, huh?

To my niece/daughter, Kandi. I am so proud of you. Thanks for honoring me with your love and laughter for all these years. Thanks for representing the family when the time came. Thanks for the hot dogs!

To my sons, Kai and Jeremy. You both do me proud. You are the reason. You have always been my reasons. Wherever you go and whatever you do, you carry my love and my soul with you. Stay strong and honorable.

## About the Author

**MS. T.** lives in a large Eastern city where, despite her obvious advantage, she continues to dabble in the art of player slaying.